Anglo-Saxon Riddles

John Porter

BY THE SAME AUTHOR

Beowulf: Text and Translation

Published by
Anglo-Saxon Books
25 Brocks Road, Swffham
Norfolk, England

PL

First published 1995
Reprinted 1996/9
Expanded and Reprinted 2003
Reprinted 2006

© John Porter

Cover illustration by Brian Partridge

A Catologuing-in-Publication record for this book is available from the British Library.

ISBN 1–898281–32-7

CONTENTS

CONTENTS

Riddles

CONTENTS

Riddles

INTRODUCTION

It is a rare culture that does not riddle, since riddle is metaphor, transformation and analogy, poetic perception, verbal play, language under creative imagination, "making it new". Whether as child's game, mythic repository, or lyric poem, as here, the riddle re-fashions vision by showing things stranger than they seem. It reveals by disguise, confuses to illumine, unifies the disparate through paradox.

For Old English poets, as for Norse skalds, this was the essence of their kennings, in which an ordinary object is transformed by analogy: *mere-hengest*, 'sea-horse', ignores the numerous ways in which a ship is entirely unlike a horse, inviting a single imaginative leap of identification. These anonymous riddles use the common alliterative and rhythmic form of Old English poetry to extend the metaphorical process, simply in some cases, such as Riddle 7, where the disguise consists mainly in the analogy between feathers and dress; densely in others, such as Riddle 12, where the diverse objects are united by the notion of their shared origin in the living animal. The result is the placing of a range of natural phenomena and human artefacts under a more or less elaborate poetic scrutiny, meditation upon which leads on to a solution not in itself of final importance since it allows and encourages further meditation on the newness of the known.

The riddles' major mode for destabilising habitual perception is the anthropomorphic, by which the inanimate is animated, given a human voice and often human features, to suggest a continual interplay between the natural and human worlds in such terms as ingenious mastery, painful necessity, paradoxes of power and submission, benefit and scourge, hunter and hunted, dumb communication, family relationship and sexual ambiguity, delivered with both humour and awe in playful patterns of language, including the use of the heathen runic letter system as an adjunct in the partially cryptographic texts (19, 24, 42, 58, 64, 75, 91).

The poems can not be firmly dated earlier than their appearance in the late tenth century Exeter Book manuscript, though the existence of riddle collections in Latin as early as the seventh century in Anglo-Saxon England allows the possibility. The Exeter Book has sustained serious damage in parts, especially towards the end, and this accounts for the fragmentary state of some riddles. My principle with the fragments has been to translate only words which are entire and to omit unintelligible letters and groups. The offered solutions represent both consensus and continuing debate. For all matters concerning the manuscript, text, emendation and debated solution the reader is referred to the three major editions of the Riddles:

Frederick Tupper Jr, *The Riddles of The Exeter Book*, 1910.
G P Krapp and E V K Dobbie, *The Exeter Book*, 1936.
Craig Williamson, *The Old English Riddles of The Exeter Book*, 1977.

Riddles

Riddle One

Hwylc is hæleþa þæs horsc   ond þæs hygecræftig
þæt þæt mæge asecgan,   hwa mec on sið wræce,
þonne ic astige strong,   stundum reþe,
þrymful þunie,   þragum wræce
5   fere geond foldan,   folcsalo bærne,
ræced reafige?   Recas stigað,
haswe ofer hrofum.   Hlin bið on eorþan,
wælcwealm wera,   þonne ic wudu hrere,
bearwas bledhwate,   beamas fylle,
10   holme gehrefed,   heahum meahtum
wrecen on waþe,   wide sended;
hæbbe me on hrycge   þæt ær hadas wreah
foldbuendra,   flæsc ond gæstas,
somod on sunde.   Saga hwa mec þecce,
15   oþþe hu ic hatte,   þe þa hlæst bere.

Riddle One

Who is a hero so bold and brainy
    as to say who spurs me on my road
when I rear up, strong, wrathful sometimes;
throbbing with thunder, thrust into exile,
I ride the world's range, rifling houses,
burning homes. Smoke rises,
grey over roofs. Earth groans
with men's dying shrieks as I shatter fruitful
woods and forests, fell standing trees.
Roofed with rain, by regal powers
sent wandering widely scattered,
on my back I bear the garments
which once hid human flesh,
as well as water. Say who swathes me,
or what I who carry that weight am called.

Riddle Two

Hwilum ic gewite,   swa ne wenaþ men,
under yþa geþræc   eorþan secan,
garsecges grund.   Gifen biþ gewreged,
fam gewealcen;
5   hwælmere hlimmeð,   hlude grimmeð,
streamas staþu beatað,   stundum weorpaþ
on stealc hleoþa   stane ond sonde,
ware ond wæge,   þonne ic winnende,
holmmægne biþeaht,   hrusan styrge,
10   side sægrundas.   Sundhelme ne mæg
losian ær mec læte   se þe min latteow bið
on siþa gehwam.   Saga, þoncol mon,
hwa mec bregde   of brimes fæþmum,
þonne streamas eft   stille weorþað,
15   yþa geþwære,   þe mec ær wrugon.

Riddle Three

Hwilum mec min frea   fæste genearwað,
sendeð þonne   under salwonges
bearm þone bradan,   ond on bid wriceð,
þrafað on þystrum   þrymma sumne,
5   hæste on enge,   þær me heord siteð
hruse on hrycge.   Nah ic hwyrftweges
of þam aglace,   ac ic eþelstol
hæleþa hrere;   hornsalu wagiað,
wera wicstede,   weallas beofiað,
10   steape ofer stiwitum.   Stille þynceð
lyft ofer londe   ond lagu swige,
oþþæt ic of enge   up aþringe,   (cont.)

Riddle Two

At times I ride beyond men's reckoning,
under beakers' crash, to seek earth,
ocean's depth. Sea is roused,
foam-tossed;
whale-mere roars, rages loudly,
waves pound headlands, sometimes hurl
on steep cliff-slopes stone and sand,
weed and water, when, wrestling,
straddled by ocean-mass, I stir the earth's
deep sea fathoms. I may not escape
my ocean-armour until the lord of all my exploits
lets me go. Say, wise man,
who raises me from flood's embrace
when streams again grow still,
the waves calm which covered me before?

Riddle Three

At times my lord tethers me tight,
sends me under fertile earth's
broad bosom and bridles me,
pens and pinions all my powers
5   harshly in darkness where hard earth
sits on my back. I can not escape
from the torment, yet shake men's
native thrones, shatter their horned gables
and buildings, buffet walls
10 steep over households. Still seems
the air over the land, and the sea is silent.
Then from bondage I burst forth,   (cont.)

13

efne swa mec wisaþ   se mec wræde on
æt frumsceafte   furþum legde,

15   bende ond clomme,   þæt ic onbugan ne mot
of þæs gewealde   þe me wegas tæcneð.
Hwilum ic sceal ufan   yþa wregan,
streamas styrgan   ond to staþe þywan
flintgrægne flod.   Famig winneð

20   wæg wið wealle,   wonn ariseð
dun ofer dype;   hyre deorc on last,
eare geblonden,   oþer fereð,
þæt hy gemittað   mearclonde neah
hea hlincas.   þær bið hlud wudu,

25   brimgiesta breahtm,   bidað stille
stealc stanhleoþu   streamgewinnes,
hopgehnastes,   þonne heah geþring
on cleofu crydeþ.   þær bið ceole wen
sliþre sæcce,   gif hine sæ byreð

30   on þa grimman tid,   gæsta fulne,
þæt he scyle rice   birofen weorþan,
feore bifohten   fæmig ridan
yþa hrycgum.   Þær bið egsa sum
ældum geywed,   þara þe ic hyran sceal

35   strong on stiðweg.   Hwa gestilleð þæt?
Hwilum ic þurhræse,   þæt me on bæce rideð
won wægfatu,   wide toþringe
lagustreama full,   hwilum læte eft
slupan tosomne.   Se bið swega mæst,

40   breahtma ofer burgum,   ond gebreca hludast,
þonne scearp cymeð   sceo wiþ oþrum,
ecg wið ecge;   earpan gesceafte
fus ofer folcum   fyre swætað,
blacan lige,   ond gebrecu ferað   (cont.)

still led by him who leashed me
from the start, restrained me
15   with fetters and shackles, unable to shake free
from the grip of him who guides my courses.
Aloft at times I must whip up the waves,
stir sea-streams, drive ashore
the flint-grey flood. Foamy strives
20   wave against cliff wall; gloomy towers
dune above the deep; dark in its track,
mingled with ocean, moves another
to their meeting with high mountains
near the land's edge. The ship is aloud
25   with sailors' cries; silently
steep stone cliffs await the strife,
when the high barrage of battering breakers
crashes on the cliffs. The ship can count on
savage conflict should the sea catch it
30   in that fierce time, freighted with souls,
to be plundered of its power,
battled out of life to ride foaming
on the torrent's ridges. The true terror
of those I must obey is laid bare to men
35   by my strong and stormy path. Who will still it?
At times I rush among dark rain-butts
riding on my back, blast far and wide
the shower-cauldrons; at times again I let them
glide together. Great is the noise
40   and tumult over cities, splitting the crash
when one cloud sharply cracks upon another,
rim against rim racing over folk,
swarthy bodies sweating fire,
bright flame; thunders prowl   (cont.)

45 deorc ofer dryhtum   gedyne micle,
farað feohtende,   feallan lætað
sweart sumsendu   seaw of bosme,
wætan of wombe.   Winnende fareð
atol eoredþreat,   egsa astigeð,
50 micel modþrea   monna cynne,
brogan on burgum,   þonne blace scotiað
scriþende scin   scearpum wæpnum.
Dol him ne ondrædeð   ða deaðsperu,
swylteð hwæþre,   gif him soð meotud
55 on geryhtu   þurh regn ufan
of gestune læteð   stræle fleogan,
farende flan.   Fea þæt gedygað,
þara þe geræceð   rynegiestes wæpen.
Ic þæs orleges   or anstelle,
60 þonne gewite   wolcengehnaste
þurh geþræc þringan   þrimme micle
ofer byrnan bosm.   Biersteð hlude
heah hloðgecrod;   þonne hnige eft
under lyfte helm   londe near,
65 ond me on hrycg hlade   þæt ic habban sceal,
meahtum gemagnad   mines frean.
Swa ic þrymful þeow   þragum winne,
hwilum under eorþan,   hwilum yþa sceal
hean underhnigan,   hwilum holm ufan
70 streamas styrge,   hwilum stige up,
wolcnfare wrege,   wide fere
swift ond swiþfeorm.   Saga hwæt ic hatte,
oþþe hwa mec rære,   þonne ic restan ne mot,
oþþe hwa mec stæðþe,   þonne ic stille beom.

45   murky above men with mighty din;
       battling they advance, from their breasts
       the jangling black juice falls,
       sap from their bellies. Battling onward
       the horrid troop stirs up hatred,
50   mighty panic among mankind,
       terror in towns, as these pallid
       gliding ghosts launch their sharp weapons.
       The fool dreads not the death-spears
       but still dies if the true Lord
55   lets fly an arrow's speeding lance
       straight down at him from the whirlwind
       through the rain. Few reached by
       the swift foe's weapon can survive.
       I start and stir up strife
60   when among massed clashing clouds
       I force my way with mighty strength
       over ocean's breast. Armed lofty ranks
       explode in uproar; then I settle
       under air's cover, near to land,
65   and load my back with its forced burden,
       admonished by the power of my prince:
       So I, a mighty slave, must fight at times,
       at times burrow in earth, at times delve below
       the ocean depths, at times disturb
70   sea-currents from above, at times climb up
       and whirl the cloud-rack, venture far and wide,
       swift and violent. Say what I am called,
       or who raises me when I may not rest,
       or who steadies me when I am still.

Riddle Four

Ic sceal þragbysig   þegne minum,
hringum hæfted,   hyran georne,
min bed brecan,   breahtme cyþan
þæt me halswriþan   hlaford sealde.
5   Oft mec slæpwerigne   secg oðþe meowle
gretan eode;   ic him gromheortum
winterceald oncweþe.   Wearm lim
gebundenne bæg   hwilum bersteð;
se þeah biþ on þonce   þegne minum,
10   medwisum men,   me þæt sylfe,
þær wiht wite,   ond wordum min
on sped mæge   spel gesecgan.

Riddle Five

Ic eom anhaga   iserne wund,
bille gebennad,   beadoweorca sæd,
ecgum werig.   Oft ic wig seo,
frecne feohtan.   Frofre ne wene,
5   þæt me geoc cyme   guðgewinnes,
ær ic mid ældum   eal forwurðe,
ac mec hnossiað   homera lafe,
heardecg heoroscearp,   hondweorc smiþa,
bitað in burgum;   ic abidan sceal
10   laþran gemotes.   Næfre læcecynn
on folcstede   findan meahte,
þara þe mid wyrtum   wunde gehælde,
ac me ecga dolg   eacen weorðað
þurh deaðslege   dagum ond nihtum.

Riddle Four

Busy and idle, fettered by rings,
I must gladly obey my master,
break my bed, stridently blazon
his gift to me - a neck chain.
My weary sleep man or woman
often broke in greeting: these enemies
I answer, wintercold. Warm limb
sometimes bursts bound fetter;
yet he is pleasing to my master,
none too wise a man; to me too,
who has some skill and in words
may triumphantly tell my tale.

Riddle Five

I am an exile, iron-wounded,
blade-battered, battle-sated,
sword-weary. War I see often,
fight foes. I fear no comfort
or help comes for me in cruel strife
before I am wrecked among warriors,
but hammered blades hack me,
hard-edged hate-sharp handwork of smiths
strikes me in strongholds; I must stay for
a crueller clash. No cure was ever
found by folk in their fields
which could heal my wounds with herbs,
but day and night through deadly blows
the swords' wounds widen in my flesh.

Riddle Six

Mec gesette soð   sigora waldend
Crist to compe.   Oft ic cwice bærne,
unrimu cyn   eorþan getenge,
næte mid niþe,   swa ic him no hrine,
5   þonne mec min frea   feohtan hateþ.
Hwilum ic monigra   mod arete,
hwilum ic frefre   þa ic ær winne on
feorran swiþe;   hi þæs felað þeah,
swylce þæs oþres,   þonne ic eft hyra
10   ofer deop gedreag   drohtað bete.

Riddle Seven

Hrægl min swigað,   þonne ic hrusan trede,
oþþe þa wic buge,   oþþe wado drefe.
Hwilum mec ahebbað   ofer hæleþa byht
hyrste mine,   ond þeos hea lyft,
5   ond mec þonne wide   wolcna strengu
ofer folc byreð.   Frætwe mine
swogað hlude   ond swinsiað,
torhte singað,   þonne ic getenge ne beom
flode ond foldan,   ferende gæst.

Riddle Six

Christ the true Lord of Triumphs
    fixed me in battle; often I burn the living,
afflict countless kins with misery
when close to earth, though I spare them
when my lord commands me to fight.
At times I gladden the hearts of many,
at times I comfort from afar
those I war upon; they feel this
as they do the other, when once more
over ocean's deep I amend their life.

Riddle Seven

Soundless my robe when I step on earth
    or rest at home or ruffle the waters.
My clothes and this lofty air
at times lift me over human dwellings,
and then clouds' power bears me
far above folk; my dress
rustles loud and whistles,
sings clearly when I am far
from flood and field, a flying spirit.

Riddle Eight

Ic þurh muþ sprece   mongum reordum,
wrencum singe,   wrixle geneahhe
heafodwoþe,   hlude cirme,
healde mine wisan,   hleoþre ne miþe,
5   eald æfensceop,   eorlum bringe
blisse in burgum,   þonne ic bugendre
stefne styrme;   stille on wicum
sittað nigende.   Saga hwæt ic hatte,
þe swa scirenige   sceawendwisan
10   hlude onhyrge,   hæleþum bodige
wilcumena fela   woþe minre.

Riddle Nine

Mec on þissum dagum   deadne ofgeafun
fæder ond modor;   ne wæs me feorh þa gen,
ealdor in innan.   Þa mec an ongon,
welhold mege,   wedum þeccan,
5   heold ond freoþode,   hleosceorpe wrah
swa arlice   swa hire agen bearn,
oþþæt ic under sceate,   swa min gesceapu wæron,
ungesibbum wearð   eacen gæste.
Mec seo friþe mæg   fedde siþþan,
10   oþþæt ic aweox,   widdor meahte
siþas asettan.   Heo hæfde swæsra þy læs
suna ond dohtra,   þy heo swa dyde.

Riddle Eight

I speak through my mouth with many voices,
chant with modulations, change my notes
frequently, cry loudly,
hold my melody, not hiding my song;
old bard of evening, I bring men
joy in their villages when with varying
voice I cry; still in the towns
they sit in silence. Say my name,
who, like a jester, loudly imitates
the minstrel's song, bidding mankind
myriad welcomes with my voice.

Riddle Nine

Left for dead in days now gone
by father and mother, no motion in me yet,
no life within; a loyal guardian
clothed me then in garments,
cherished and nourished me, wrapped me in robes
as kindly as her own kin,
until under her breast, blessed by fate,
I grew strong in spirit among strangers.
My fair foster-mother fed me then
until maturity and management
of wider journeys. She had fewer loved
sons and daughters by doing this.

Riddle Ten

Neb wæs min on nearwe,   ond ic neoþan wætre,
flode underflowen,   firgenstreamum
swiþe besuncen,   ond on sunde awox
ufan yþum þeaht,   anum getenge
5   liþendum wuda   lice mine.
Hæfde feorh cwico,   þa ic of fæðmum cwom
brimes ond beames   on blacum hrægle;
sume wæron hwite   hyrste mine,
þa mec lifgende   lyft upp ahof,
10   wind of wæge,   siþþan wide bær
ofer seolhbaþo.   Saga hwæt ic hatte.

Riddle Eleven

Hrægl is min hasofag,   hyrste beorhte,
reade ond scire   on reafe minum.
Ic dysge dwelle   ond dole hwette
unrædsiþas,   oþrum styre
5   nyttre fore.   Ic þæs nowiht wat
þæt heo swa gemædde,   mode bestolene,
dæde gedwolene,   deoraþ mine
won wisan gehwam.   Wa him þæs þeawes,
siþþan heah bringað   horda deorast,
10   gif hi unrædes   ær ne geswicaþ.

24

Riddle Ten

My beak was narrow, and below water,
by flood under-flowed, in ocean currents
deeply sunk in sea I sprouted,
covered by waves above, clinging to
floating timber with my body.
·I burst to life when from the lap
of brine and branch I came in black robe;
some of my plumes were white
when living air lifted me up,
wind out of wave, then widely bore me
over seal's bath. Say what I am called.

Riddle Eleven

My coat is dark, my dress bright,
red and gleaming in my garments.
I fool the foolish and urge the silly
on unwise journeys; others I steer
on a useful path. I know not why
they, thus maddened, mind-stolen,
deed-perverse, should praise
my crooked ways to all. Woe to them in their acts,
when they bring their precious hoards on high,
if they from folly have not yet refrained.

Riddle Twelve

Fotum ic fere,   foldan slite,
grene wongas,   þenden ic gæst bere.
Gif me feorh losað,   fæste binde
swearte Wealas,   hwilum sellan men.
5   Hwilum ic deorum   drincan selle
beorne of bosme,   hwilum mec bryd triedeð
felawlonc fotum,   hwilum feorran broht
wonfeax Wale   wegeð ond þyð,
dol druncmennen   deorcum nihtum,
10   wæteð in wætre,   wyrmeð hwilum
fægre to fyre;   me on fæðme sticaþ
hygegalan hond,   hwyrfeð geneahhe,
swifeð me geond sweartne.   Saga hwæt ic hatte,
þe ic lifgende   lond reafige
15   ond æfter deaþe   dryhtum þeowige.

Riddle Thirteen

Ic seah turf tredan,   X wæron ealra,
VI gebroþor   ond hyra sweostor mid;
hæfdon feorg cwico.   Fell hongedon
sweotol ond gesyne   on seles wæge
5   anra gehwylces.   Ne wæs hyra ængum þy wyrs,
ne siðe þy sarre,   þeah hy swa sceoldon
reafe birofene,   rodra weardes
meahtum aweahte,   muþum slitan
haswe blede.   Hrægl bið geniwad
10   þam þe ær forðcymene   frætwe leton
licgan on laste,   gewitan lond tredan.

Riddle Twelve

A foot I fare furrowing earth,
  green fields, while my spirit lives.
When life fails me I bind fast
swarthy Welshmen, sometimes their betters.
Now to brave soldier I give suck
from my breast; now bride treads
me with haughty foot; now dark-haired
far-ferried Welsh girl holds and fondles me,
dulled by drink in dark of night,
wets me with water, now warms me
fitly at the fire, thrusts fingers
lustfully in my lap, loves to twirl me,
strokes me through the dark. Say what I am called,
who, living, plunders land,
and after death does duty for mankind.

Riddle Thirteen

I saw them treading turf, they were ten in all,
  six brothers and their sisters too,
they had life's spark. The skins of each
hung clear and visible on the hall's wall.
None of them was the worse off
nor more troubled on their travels, even though,
stripped of shell, strength awakened
by heaven's guardian, they must with mouths rend
dark leaves. Robes are renewed
for them who, newly emerged, left coats
lying in their track, setting out to tread the land.

Riddle Fourteen

Ic wæs wæpenwiga.   Nu mec wlonc þeceð
geong hagostealdmon   golde ond sylfore,
woum wirbogum.   Hwilum weras cyssað,
hwilum ic to hilde   hleoþre bonne
5   wilgehleþan,   hwilum wycg byreþ
mec ofer mearce,   hwilum merehengest
fereð ofer flodas   frætwum beorhtne,
hwilum mægða sum   minne gefylleð
bosm beaghroden;   hwilum ic bordum sceal,
10   heard, heafodleas,   behlyþed licgan,
hwilum hongige   hyrstum frætwed,
wlitig on wage,   þær weras drincað,
freolic fyrdsceorp.   Hwilum folcwigan
on wicge wegað,   þonne ic winde sceal
15   sincfag swelgan   of sumes bosme;
hwilum ic gereordum   rincas laðige
wlonce to wine;   hwilum wraþum sceal
stefne minre   forstolen hreddan,
flyman feondsceaþan.   Frige hwæt ic hatte.

Riddle Fourteen

I was an armed fighter. Now the proud young
warrior garbs me in gold and silver,
whirls of twisted wire. Now men kiss me,
now with my song I summon
comrades to battle; now horse bears me
over marches; now sea-stallion
ferries me over ocean, flashing with jewels;
now some ring-decked girl
fills my brown depths; now on boards I must lie,
hard, headless, stripped bare;
now I hang adorned with finery,
fair on the wall where warriors drink,
splendid war-gear. Now soldiers
bear me on horseback, when from one's breast,
shining with treasure, I swallow wind;
now with my notes I summon noble
warriors to wine; now from robbers I must
with my voice recover plunder,
put foes to flight. Find out my name.

Hals is min hwit   ond heafod fealo,
sidan swa some.   Swift ic eom on feþe,
beadowæpen bere.   Me on bæce standað
her swylce swe on hleorum.   Hlifiað tu
5   earan ofer eagum.   Ordum ic steppe
in grene græs.   Me bið gyrn witod,
gif mec onhæle   an onfindeð
wælgrim wiga,   þær ic wic buge,
bold mid bearnum,   ond ic bide þær
10   mid geoguðcnosle,   hwonne gæst cume
to durum minum,   him biþ deað witod.
Forþon ic sceal of eðle   eaforan mine
forhtmod fergan,   fleame nergan,
gif he me æfterweard   ealles weorþeð;
15   hine berað breost.   Ic his bidan ne dear,
reþes on geruman,   (nele þæt ræd teale),
ac ic sceal fromlice   feþemundum
þurh steapne beorg   stræte wyrcan.
Eaþe ic mæg freora   feorh genergan,
20   gif ic mægburge mot   mine gelædan
on degolne weg   þurh dune þyrel
swæse ond gesibbe;   ic me siþþan ne þearf
wælhwelpes wig   wiht onsittan.
Gif se niðsceaþa   nearwe stige
25   me on swaþe seceþ,   ne tosæleþ him
on þam gegnpaþe   guþgemotes,
siþþan ic þurh hylles   hrof geræce,
ond þurh hest hrino   hildepilum
laðgewinnum,   þam þe ic longe fleah.

Riddle Fifteen

My neck is white, and head grey,
sides the same. Swift am I in motion,
bear a battle-weapon. On my back hair
bristles, so too on cheeks. Two ears tower
over my eyes. On toes I step
in green grass. Grief is fated for me
if some death-fierce fighter
finds me hidden where I dwell in den,
in lair with my litter, and if I lurk there
with my brood when foe comes
to my doors, death will be their lot.
So I must boldly bear my heirs
from home, save them in flight,
if he chases me in close pursuit;
he hunts on his belly. I dare not bide his
fury in my covert, can not think it wise,
but fast with forepaws I must
make a street through steep hill.
With ease I may save my loved ones' lives
if I might lead my family
on a hidden path through hill's hole,
my kith and kin; then I will not need
in any way to dread death-dog's attack.
If the deadly foe through narrow way
seeks out my track, he will not lack
a battle-meeting on the path of war,
when I reach out through hill's roof
and fiercely strike with battle-spears
the hated foe whom I long fled.

Riddle Sixteen

Oft ic sceal wiþ wæge winnan ond wiþ winde feohtan,
somod wið þam sæcce, þonne ic secan gewite
eorþan yþum þeaht; me biþ se eþel fremde.
Ic beom strong þæs gewinnes, gif ic stille weorþe;
5   gif me þæs tosæleð, hi beoð swiþran þonne ic,
ond mec slitende sona flymað,
willað oþfergan þæt ic friþian sceal.
Ic him þæt forstonde, gif min steort þolað
ond mec stiþne wiþ stanas moton
10   fæste gehabban. Frige hwæt ic hatte.

Riddle Seventeen

Ic eom mundbora minre heorde,
eodorwirum fæst, innan gefylled
dryhtgestreona. Dægtidum oft
spæte sperebrogan; sped biþ þy mare
5   fylle minre. Frea þæt bihealdeð,
hu me of hrife fleogað hyldepilas.
Hwilum ic sweartum swelgan onginne
brunum beadowæpnum, bitrum ordum,
eglum attorsperum. Is min innað til,
10   wombhord wlitig, wloncum deore;
men gemunan þæt me þurh muþ fareð.

Riddle Sixteen

Often I must wrestle with waves and fight with wind,
tussle them both together when, thatched with billows,
I dive to seek the depth, a stranger in my homeland.
I am strong in the struggle if I grow still;
if I fail in that, their force outweighs mine
and, wrenching me, they rout me instantly,
want to fetch off what I must fasten.
I can resist them if my root holds
and stones may stoutly keep me firm
against their force. Find out my name.

Riddle Seventeen

I am the father of my flock,
a fence of firm wires filled
with dear treasures. By day I often
spit out spear-dread; I prosper the more
for my fullness. The lord beholds
how from my belly fly the battle-shafts.
Sometimes I swallow swart
brown weapons, bitter tips,
piercing spears of poison. My paunch is good,
a womb stuffed with wonders dear to warriors;
men remember what issues through my mouth.

Riddle Eighteen

Ic eom wunderlicu wiht;   ne mæg word sprecan,
mældan for monnum,   þeah ic muþ hæbbe,
wide wombe
Ic wæs on ceole   ond mines cnosles ma.

Riddle Nineteen

Ic on siþe seah   ᚻᚱᚠ
ᚾ hygewloncne,   heafodbeorhtne,
swiftne ofer sælwong   swiþe þrægan.
Hæfde him on hrycge   hildeþryþe
5   ᛏᚠᛗ nægledne rad
ᚠᚷᛖᚹ Widlast ferede
rynestrong on rade   rofne ᚳᚠ
ᚹᚠᚠᚾ For wæs þy beorhtre,
swylcra siþfæt.   Saga hwæt ic hatte.

Riddle Eighteen

I am a curious creature; can not speak words
or talk to men, though a mouth I have,
a broad belly
I was in a ship and more of my kinsmen.

Riddle Nineteen

Journeying I saw S. R. O.
H.[1] thought-proud, head-bright,
swift over fertile plains strong running.
Had on his back war-strength
N. O. M.[2] nailed R.
A. G. E. W.[3] Wide-wandering he bore
road-strong in riding bold C. O.
F. O. A. H.[4] His route was the richer
for such splendour. Say my name.

[1] HORS horse
[2] MON man
[3] WEGAR war-spear
[4] HAOFOC hawk

Riddle Twenty

Ic eom wunderlicu wiht,   on gewin sceapen,
frean minum leof,   fægre gegyrwed.
Byrne is min bleofag,   swylce beorht seomað
wir ymb þone wælgim   þe me waldend geaf,
5   se me widgalum   wisað hwilum
sylfum to sace.   þonne ic sinc wege
þurh hlutterne dæg,   hondweorc smiþa,
gold ofer geardas.   Oft ic gæstberend
cwelle compwæpnum.   Cyning mec gyrweð
10   since ond seolfre   ond mec on sele weorþað;
ne wyrneð wordlofes,   wisan mæneð
mine for mengo,   þær hy meodu drincað,
healdeð mec on heaþore,   hwilum læteð eft
radwerigne   on gerum sceacan,
15   orlegfromne.   Oft ic oþrum scod
frecne æt his freonde;   fah eom ic wide,
wæpnum awyrged.   Ic me wenan ne þearf
þæt me bearn wræce   on bonan feore,
gif me gromra hwylc   guþe genægeð;
20   ne weorþeð sio mægburg   gemicledu
eaforan minum   þe ic æfter woc,
nymþe ic hlafordleas   hweorfan mote
from þam healdende   þe me hringas geaf.
Me bið forð witod,   gif ic frean hyre,
25   guþe fremme,   swa ic gien dyde
minum þeodne on þonc,   þæt ic þolian sceal
bearngestreona.   Ic wiþ bryde ne mot
hæmed habban,   ac me þæs hyhtplegan
geno wyrneð,   se mec geara on   (cont.)

Riddle Twenty

I am a strange thing, forged in strife,
dear to my lord, finely adorned.
My mail is mottled and bright wire twines
the death-gem which my ruler gave me,
who, in his wanderings, wields me himself
at times in strife. Then I wear treasure
through the bright day, handwork of smiths,
gold among courts. Often I kill
living men with battle-weapons. King adorns me
with treasure and silver, and honours me in hall,
showers praise, shouts my virtues
to the throng where they drink mead;
holds me in check, at times lets me again
go free, travel-weary,
strong in battle. Often in his friend's hands
I hurt others harshly; I am widely hated,
damned by weapons. I need not hope
that a son will avenge me on my slayer's life
should some enemy attack me in battle;
the stock from which I'm sprung
is swelled by no child of mine,
unless, lordless, I might leave
the guardian who gave me rings.
If I obey my lord, wage war
as I did before for my prince's pleasure,
my lot is cast that I must lack
the blessing of children. With bride I may not
please my flesh, for he who first
laid bonds on me still bans   (cont.)

30 bende legde; forþon ic brucan sceal
    on hagostealde hæleþa gestreona.
    Oft ic wirum dol wife abelge,
    wonie hyre willan; heo me wom spreceð,
    floceð hyre folmum, firenaþ mec wordum,
35 ungod gæleð. Ic ne gyme þæs compes

Riddle Twenty-one

    Neb is min niþerweard; neol ic fere
    ond be grunde græfe, geonge swa me wisað
    har holtes feond, ond hlaford min
    woh færeð weard æt steorte,
5   wrigaþ on wonge, wegeð mec ond þyð,
    saweþ on swæð min. Ic snyþige forð,
    brungen of bearwe, bunden cræfte,
    wegen on wægne, hæbbe wundra fela;
    me biþ gongendre grene on healfe
10 ond min swæð sweotol sweart on oþre.
    Me þurh hrycg wrecen hongaþ under
    an orþoncpil, oþer on heafde,
    fæst ond forðweard. Fealleþ on sidan
    þæt ic toþum tere, gif me teala þenaþ
15 hindeweardre, þæt biþ hlaford min.

me that merry game; therefore I must as a
bachelor enjoy the treasures of heroes.
Often, a fool in filigree, I anger a woman,
thwart her desire; she rails at me,
claps her hands, scolds me in words,
screeches evil. I care not for that contest.

Riddle Twenty-one

My beak bends down; deep I travel
and engrave ground, go as the grey
forest foe guides me, and my master,
the guard at my tail, goes stooping,
wrenches, thrusts and drives me through the field,
sows in my wake. I snuffle forth,
brought from the wood, bound skilfully,
fetched by wagon, I am full of wonders;
on one side my track is green
and my trail pure black on the other.
Driven through my spine a skilful spear
hangs down, in my head another,
fixed and forward-jutting. What I tear with teeth
falls aside if from behind
he who is my master serves me well.

Ætsomne cwom   *LX* monna
to wægstæþe   wicgum ridan;
hæfdon *XI*   eoredmæcgas
fridhengestas,   *IIII* sceamas.

5   Ne meahton magorincas   ofer mere feolan,
swa hi fundedon,   ac wæs flod to deop,
atol yþa geþræc,   ofras hea,
streamas stronge.   Ongunnon stigan þa
on wægn weras   ond hyra wicg somod

10   hlodan under hrunge;   þa þa hors oðbær
eh ond eorlas,   æscum dealle,
ofer wætres byht   wægn to lande,
swa hine oxa ne teah   ne esna mægen
ne fæthengest,   ne on flode swom,

15   ne be grunde wod   gestum under,
ne lagu drefde,   ne on lyfte fleag,
ne under bæc cyrde;   brohte hwæþre
beornas ofer burnan   ond hyra bloncan mid
from stæðe heaum,   þæt hy stopan up

20   on oþerne,   ellenrofe,
weras of wæge,   ond hyra wicg gesund.

Riddle Twenty-two

S ixty men together came
to sea-shore riding horses;
eleven horsemen had
steeds of peace, four of them white.
The company could not cross the sea
as they desired, for the flood was too deep,
frightful the waves' force, shores high,
streams strong. The men stepped aboard
a wagon then and loaded their mounts
together under the ridge-beam; then it bore
off horses, steeds and men proud with spears,
wagon across water's home to land;
no ox drew it, nor asses' strength
nor sturdy dray, nor did it swim the flood,
nor waded ocean's bed beneath its guests,
nor stirred the sea, nor flew in air
nor turned back; yet it brought
heroes over burn and their horses too
from the high shore, so that they landed safe
on the other bank, the bold riders
and their mounts, warriors from the wave.

Riddle Twenty-three

Agof is min noma   eft onhwyrfed;
ic eom wrætlic wiht   on gewin sceapen.
þonne ic onbuge,   ond me of bosme fareð
ætren onga,   ic beom eallgearo
5   þæt ic me þæt feorhbealo   feor aswape.
Siþþan me se waldend,   se me þæt wite gescop,
leoþo forlæteð,   ic beo lengre þonne ær,
oþþæt ic spæte,   spilde geblonden,
ealfelo attor   þæt ic ær geap.
10   Ne togongeð þæs   gumena hwylcum,
ænigum eaþe   þæt ic þær ymb sprice;
gif hine hrineð   þæt me of hrife fleogeð,
þæt þone mandrinc   mægne geceapaþ,
fullwered fæste   feore sine.
15   Nelle ic unbunden   ænigum hyran
nymþe searosæled.   Saga hwæt ic hatte.

Riddle Twenty-four

Ic eom wunderlicu wiht,   wræsne mine stefne,
hwilum beorce swa hund,   hwilum blæte swa gat,
hwilum græde swa gos,   hwilum gielle swa hafoc,
hwilum ic onhyrge   þone haswan earn,
5   guðfugles hleoþor,   hwilum glidan reorde
muþe gemæne,   hwilum mæwes song,
þær ic glado sitte.   ☓ mec nemnað,
swylce ᚠ ond ᚱ   fullesteð,
ᚻ ond ᛁ   Nu ic haten eom
10   swa þa siex stafas   sweotule becnaþ.

Riddle Twenty-three

A GOF is my name back to front;
 I am a strange thing shaped in strife.
When I bend, and from my breast flies
poison sting, I quiver
to launch the lethal evil far from me.
When the ruler who racked me with pain
releases my limbs I am longer than before,
until, stuffed with suffering, I spit
the deadly venom that I drank before.
No man is healed easily
from the harm I speak of;
if what hurtles from my belly hits him
he buys the fatal drink with his strength,
lasting atonement with his life.
Unbound I will obey no man,
unless cunningly strung. Say what I'm called.

Riddle Twenty-four

I am a curious creature, change my voice,
 now bark like dog, now bleat like goat,
now screech like goose, now scream like hawk,
now I ape the dusky eagle,
war-bird's cry, now with kite's call
in mouth I speak, now sea-gull's song,
where I sit in joy. G they name me,
so too Æ and R, O supports,
H and I. Now I am known
as these six staves clearly show.

Ic eom wunderlicu wiht,   wifum on hyhte,
neahbuendum nyt;   nængum sceþþe
burgsittendra,   nymþe bonan anum.
Staþol min is steapheah,   stonde ic on bedde,
5   neoþan ruh nathwær.   Neþeð hwilum
ful cyrtenu   ceorles dohtor,   .
modwlonc meowle,   þæt heo on mec gripeð,
ræseð mec on reodne,   reafað min heafod,
fegeð mec on fæsten.   Feleþ sona
10   mines gemotes,   seo þe mec nearwað,
wif wundenlocc.   Wæt bið þæt eage.

Riddle Twenty-five

I am a wondrous thing, woman's delight,
handy in the home; I harm no
householder but him who hurts me.
My stalk is tall, I stand in bed,
my root rather hairy. The haughty girl,
churl's gorgeous daughter,
sometimes has courage to clasp me,
rushes my redness, rapes my head,
stows me in her stronghold. Straightway
the curly-locked lady who clamps me
weeps at our wedding. Wet is her eye.

Mec feonda sum   feore besnyþede,
woruldstrenga binom,   wætte siþþan,
dyfde on wætre,   dyde eft þonan,
sette on sunnan,   þær ic swiþe beleas
5   herum þam þe ic hæfde.   Heard mec siþþan
snað seaxses ecg,   sindrum begrunden;
fingras feoldan,   ond mec fugles wyn
geond speddropum   spyrede geneahhe,
ofer brunne brerd,   beamtelge swealg,
10   streames dæle,   stop eft on mec,
siþade sweartlast.   Mec siþþan wrah
hæleð hleobordum,   hyde beþenede,
gierede mec mid golde;   forþon me gliwedon
wrætlic weorc smiþa,   wire bifongen.
15   Nu þa gereno   ond se reada telg
ond þa wuldorgesteald   wide mære
dryhtfolca helm,   nales dol wite.
Gif min bearn wera   brucan willað,
hy beoð þy gesundran   ond þy sigefæstran,
20   heortum þy hwætran   ond þy hygebliþran,
ferþe þy frodran,   habbaþ freonda þy ma,
swæsra ond gesibbra,   soþra ond godra,
tilra ond getreowra,   þa hyra tyr ond ead
estum ycað   ond hy arstafum
25   lissum bilecgað   ond hi lufan fæþmum
fæste clyppað.   Frige hwæt ic hatte,
niþum to nytte.   Nama min is mære,
hæleþum gifre   ond halig sylf.

Riddle Twenty-six

Some enemy stole my life,
deprived me of power, plunged and
wetted me in water, whisked me out,
set me in sun where I soon lost
what hair I had. Honed edge
of harsh knife hacked me then,
fingers folded me, and feather often
spread jets of useful juice
over my brown body, sipped wood-dye
with a dash of water, walked back on me,
went on its black way. Then a man
bound hide over boards to shield me,
adorned me with gold; gleaming wire
entwines the cunning work of craftsmen.
Now far and wide the riches and the red dye
and the gorgeous jewels glorify
the shield of peoples, not the pains of hell.
 If men's sons will make good use of me
they will be sounder and surer of victory,
bolder in heart and happier in thought,
wiser in spirit, win more friends,
kinsmen and cousins close and true,
honest and loyal, eager to increase
their fame and honour, heap them
with joys and favours and fold them
in love's firm embrace. Find my title,
a boon to humans. My name is famous,
a help to heroes, and itself holy.

Riddle Twenty-seven

Ic eom weorð werum,　wide funden,
brungen of bearwum　ond of burghleoþum,
of denum ond of dunum.　Dæges mec wægun
feþre on lifte,　feredon mid liste
5　under hrofes hleo.　Hæleð mec siþþan
baþedan in bydene.　Nu ic eom bindere
ond swingere,　sona weorpe
esne to eorþan,　hwilum ealdne ceorl.
Sona þæt onfindeð,　se þe mec fehð ongean,
10　ond wið mægenþisan　minre genæsteð,
þæt he hrycge sceal　hrusan secan,
gif he unrædes　ær ne geswiceð,
strengo bistolen,　strong on spræce,
mægene binumen;　nah his modes geweald,
15　fota ne folma.　Frige hwæt ic hatte,
ðe on eorþan swa　esnas binde,
dole æfter dyntum　be dæges leohte.

Riddle Twenty-seven

I am men's wealth, widely found,
fetched from forests and fell-slopes,
from dales and downs. By day wings
bore me in air, artfully brought me
under roof's shelter. Men soaked me
then in a barrel. Now I am binder
and flail, fling green youth
straight to ground, and greybeards too.
He who struggles with me and strives
against my power, still persisting
in his folly, soon finds out
that his back must bite earth,
stripped of strength, strident in speech,
robbed of might; he can master neither mind
nor foot nor hand. Find my name,
who thus by light of day on earth
can bind men dulled by blows.

Riddle Twenty-eight

Biþ foldan dæl   fægre gegierwed
mid þy heardestan   ond mid þy scearpestan
ond mid þy grymmestan   gumena gestreona,
corfen, sworfen,   cyrred, þyrred,
5   bunden, wunden,   blæced, wæced,
frætwed, geatwed,   feorran læded
to durum dryhta.   Dream bið in innan
cwicra wihta,   clengeð, lengeð,
þara þe ær lifgende   longe hwile
10   wilna bruceð   ond no wið spriceð,
ond þonne æfter deaþe   deman onginneð,
meldan mislice.   Micel is to hycganne
wisfæstum menn,   hwæt seo wiht sy.

Riddle Twenty-nine

Ic wiht geseah   wundorlice
hornum bitweonum   huþe lædan,
lyftfæt leohtlic,   listum gegierwed,
huþe to þam ham   of þam heresiþe;
5   walde hyre on þære byrig   bur atimbran,
searwum asettan,   gif hit swa meahte.
ða cwom wundorlicu wiht   ofer wealles hrof,
seo is eallum cuð   eorðbuendum,
ahredde þa þa huþe   ond to ham bedraf
10   wreccan ofer willan,   gewat hyre west þonan
fæhþum feran,   forð onette.
Dust stonc to heofonum,   deaw feol on eorþan,
niht forð gewat.   Nænig siþþan
wera gewiste   þære wihte sið.

50

Riddle Twenty-eight

A region of earth is richly endowed
with the hardest and with the sharpest
and with the fiercest of men's fortunes,
carved, polished, wried, dried,
bound, wound, bleached, leached,
burnished, furnished, brought from afar
to men's houses. Human happiness
is stored inside it; it strengthens, lengthens
the days of those already long-lived,
who enjoy their desires, not denying them,
and then after its strength fades, start to judge
with differing opinions. There is much to ponder
for the wise man, what this thing is.

Riddle Twenty-nine

I saw a curious creature,
radiant sky-rider richly adorned,
bearing booty between its horns,
returning home with its war-haul,
planning a sanctuary in the city,
artful architecture if it might.
Then a miracle rose above the roof,
well-known to all earth-dwellers,
rescued the spoils and routed
the unwilling exile, wandered westwards,
sped victorious in vengeance.
Dust rose to heaven, dew fell on earth,
night departed. No man knew
the creature's course thereafter.

Riddle Thirty

Ic eom ligbysig,   lace mid winde,
bewunden mid wuldre,   wedre gesomnad,
fus forðweges,   fyre gebysgad,
bearu blowende,   byrnende gled.
5   Ful oft mec gesiþas   sendað æfter hondum,
þær mec weras ond wif   wlonce gecyssað.
Þonne ic mec onhæbbe,   hi onhnigað to me,
monige mid miltse,   þær ic monnum sceal
ycan upcyme   eadignesse.

Riddle Thirty-one

Is þes middangeard   missenlicum
wisum gewlitegad,   wrættum gefrætwad.
Ic seah sellic þing   singan on ræcede;
wiht wæs nower   werum on gemonge,
5   sio hæfde wæstum   wundorlicran.
Niþerweard   wæs neb hyre,
fet ond folme   fugele gelice;
no hwæþre fleogan mæg   ne fela gongan,
hwæþre feþegeorn   fremman onginneð,
10   gecoren cræftum,   cyrreð geneahhe
oft ond gelome   eorlum on gemonge,
siteð æt symble,   sæles bideþ,
hwonne ær heo cræft hyre   cyþan mote
werum on wonge.   Ne heo þær wiht þigeð
     15   þæs þe him æt blisse   beornas habbað.
Deor domes georn,   hio dumb wunað;   (cont.)

52

Riddle Thirty

I flicker like fire, flirt with wind,
swathed in splendour, tossed in storm,
eager on journeys, eaten by flame,
a blossoming grove, a burning gleed.
Friends often pass me from hand to hand
for worthy men and women to kiss me.
Where I rise up and they reverently bow
to me in throngs, there I shall enrich
men's destiny and their souls' delight.

Riddle Thirty-one

In countless ways this world is
ornamented with exotic wonders.
I saw a strange thing singing in a hall.
There was nowhere a creature among men
which had a form more fantastic.
A beak which droops,
feet and hands like a bird,
but she can not take wing nor walk at all,
yet, straining to be off, she starts to move;
polished in arts, she passes back
and forth among fellows,
sits at banquet, bides her time
until she can display her skill
to mankind. She eats no morsel
of what men have at their merrymaking.
Loved, questing fame, she stays dumb;   (cont.)

hwæþre hyre is on fote   fæger hleoþor,
wynlicu woðgiefu.   Wrætlic me þinceð,
hu seo wiht mæge   wordum lacan
20   þurh fot neoþan,   frætwed hyrstum.
Hafað hyre on halse,   þonne hio hord wa128ð,
bær, beagum deall,   broþor sine,
mæg mid mægne.   Micel is to hycgenne
wisum woðboran,   hwæt sio wiht sie

Riddle Thirty-two

Is þes middangeard   missenlicum
wisum gewlitegad,   wrættum gefrætwad.
Siþum sellic   ic seah searo hweorfan,
grindan wið greote,   giellende faran.
5   Næfde sellicu wiht   syne ne folme,
exle ne earmas;   sceal on anum fet
searoceap swifan,   swiþe feran,
faran ofer feldas.   Hæfde fela ribba;
muð wæs on middan.   Moncynne nyt,
10   fereð foddurwelan,   folcscipe dreogeð,
wist in wigeð,   ond werum gieldeð
gaful geara gehwam   þæs þe guman brucað,
rice ond heane.   Rece, gif þu cunne,
wis worda gleaw,   hwæt sio wiht sie.

yet in her foot there is a fine voice,
glorious gift of song. Strange to me
how the creature can conjure speech
through a finely ornamented foot.
Her brothers, ranks of kinsmen, wreathe
her naked neck with rings
when she wears jewels. Wise poets
must long ponder who this lady is.

Riddle Thirty-two

In countless ways this world
is ornamented with exotic wonders.
I saw a travel-skilled gadget screech
its grinding road through gravel.
The artful thing had neither eyes nor hands,
shoulders nor arms; on one foot must
this queer device furrow its fields
in mighty journeys. It had many ribs,
a mouth in its midriff. Man's helper,
it ferries food-wealth to folk,
carries to king and commoner
a yield of useful goods
in yearly tribute. Tell if you can,
man wise in words, what this thing is.

Riddle Thirty-three

Wiht cwom æfter wege   wrætlicu liþan,
cymlic from ceole   cleopode to londe,
hlinsade hlude;   hleahtor wæs gryrelic,
egesful on earde,   ecge wæron scearpe.
5   Wæs hio hetegrim,   hilde to sæne,
biter beadoweorca;   bordweallas grof,
heardhiþende.   Heterune bond,
sægde searocræftig   ymb hyre sylfre gesceaft:
"Is min modor   mægða cynnes
10   þæs deorestan,   þæt is dohtor min
eacen up liden,   swa þæt is ældum cuþ,
firum on folce,   þæt seo on foldan sceal
on ealra londa gehwam   lissum stondan."

Riddle Thirty-four

Ic wiht geseah   in wera burgum,
seo þæt feoh fedeð.   Hafað fela toþa;
nebb biþ hyre æt nytte,   niþerweard gongeð,
hiþeð holdlice   ond to ham tyhð,
5   wæþeð geond weallas,   wyrte seceð;
aa heo þa findeð,   þa þe fæst ne biþ;
læteð hio þa wlitigan,   wyrtum fæste,
stille stondan   on staþolwonge,
beorhte blican,   blowan ond growan.

Riddle Thirty-three

S he came sailing weirdly through the waves,
shouted in splendour from ship to shore,
booming loudly, her laughter terrible,
awesome on earth, edges like swords.
She was savage with hate, slow to strike,
bloody in battle; battered ships' ribs,
ravaged harshly. She knotted riddles,
spoke in spells about her own spawning:
"My mother is a maiden of
purest descent, she is my daughter,
swollen with growth, greeted by folk
where she falls on fields of earth,
blessing the lands where men live."

Riddle Thirty-four

I saw a strange thing in men's strongholds
feeding cattle. Crammed with teeth,
its useful beak is bent down;
it roams through plots, seeking plants,
raids them swiftly and returns home;
it always ferrets out the frail,
leaves the fine ones firmly rooted
standing still on their stalks
brightly blooming, glowing and growing.

Riddle Thirty-five

Mec se wæta wong,   wundrum freorig,
of his innaþe   ærist cende.
Ne wat ic mec beworhtne   wulle flysum,
hærum þurh heahcræft,   hygeþoncum min.
5   Wundene me ne beoð wefle,   ne ic wearp hafu,
ne þurh þreata geþræcu   þræd me ne hlimmeð,
ne æt me hrutende   hrisil scriþeð,
ne mec ohwonan   sceal am cnyssan.
Wyrmas mec ne awæfan   wyrda cræftum,
10   þa þe geolo godwebb   geatwum frætwað.
Wile mec mon hwæþre seþeah   wide ofer eorþan
hatan for hæleþum   hyhtlic gewæde.
Saga soðcwidum,   searoþoncum gleaw,
wordum wisfæst,   hwæt þis gewæde sy.

Riddle Thirty-six

Ic wiht geseah   on wege feran,
seo wæs wrætlice   wundrum gegierwed.
Hæfde feowere   fet under wombe
ond ehtuwe   ufon on hrycge;
5   hæfde tu fiþru   ond twelf eagan
ond siex heafdu.   Saga hwæt hio wære.
For flodwegas;   ne wæs þæt na fugul ana,
ac þær wæs æghwylces   anra gelicnes
horses ond monnes,   hundes ond fugles,
10   ond eac wifes wlite.   þu wast, gif þu const,
to gesecganne,   þæt we soð witan,
hu þære wihte   wise gonge.

Riddle Thirty-five

The drenched acre of earth first
fathered me out of its frozen womb.
My mind knows I was not knit
from woollen fleece or twined from hair.
No weft was woven in me, no warp I have,
no throngs of thread sang my tissue,
no whirring shuttle snaked my flesh
nor loom-bar laced me with its blows.
Worms' weird skill did not weave me,
spinning beauty in their golden webs.
Yet all over earth I am honoured,
held in heroes' high esteem.
Thought-skilled men, thoroughly wise
in words, will guess this garment's name.

Riddle Thirty-six

I saw a beast breasting the waves,
it was strangely stuffed with wonders.
It had four feet beneath its belly
and eight upon its back;
had two wings, twelve eyes
and six heads. Say what it was.
It flew over oceans but was no bird,
yet showed some likeness to
horse and man, hound and bird,
and woman's beauty too. You will, if you know
how to, tell the truth about
the way in which this creature moves.

Riddle Thirty-seven

Ic þa wihte geseah;   womb wæs on hindan
þriþum aþrunten.   Þegn folgade,
mægenrofa man,   ond micel hæfde
gefered þæt hit felde,   fleah þurh his eage.
5   Ne swylteð he symle,   þonne syllan sceal
innað þam oþrum,   ac him eft cymeð
bot in bosme,   blæd biþ aræred;
he sunu wyrceð,   bið him sylfa fæder.

Riddle Thirty-eight

Ic þa wiht geseah   wæpnedcynnes,
geoguðmyrþe grædig;   him on gafol forlet
ferðfriþende   feower wellan
scire sceotan,   on gesceap þeotan.
5   Mon maþelade,   se þe me gesægde:
"Seo wiht, gif hio gedygeð,   duna briceð;
gif he tobirsteð,   bindeð cwice."

Riddle Thirty-seven

I saw the beast; his belly bulging
hugely on his back. A bold man
served him with strength, his stomach's
filling flew out through his eye.
He never dies when he must spill
his guts for others, but a cure creeps
back to his breast, and breath revives;
he fathers sons, the fathers of himself.

Riddle Thirty-eight

I saw a beast bristling with weapons,
greedy with the glee of youth; he tugged tribute
from four life-giving fountains
brightly jetting, drizzling delight.
A man spoke and said to me:
"If he lives this beast will break fields,
if he dies, will bind the living."

Gewritu secgað   þæt seo wiht sy
mid moncynne   miclum tidum
sweotol ond gesyne.   Sundorcræft hafað
maran micle,   þonne hit men witen.
5   Heo wile gesecan   sundor æghwylcne
feorhberendra,   gewiteð eft feran on weg.
Ne bið hio næfre   niht þær oþre,
ac hio sceal wideferh   wreccan laste
hamleas hweorfan;   no þy heanre biþ.
10   Ne hafað hio fot ne folme,   ne æfre foldan hran,
ne eagena   ægþer twega,
ne muð hafaþ,   ne wiþ monnum spræc,
ne gewit hafað,   ac gewritu secgað
þæt seo sy earmost   ealra wihta,
15   þara þe æfter gecyndum   cenned wære.
Ne hafað hio sawle ne feorh,   ac hio siþas sceal
geond þas wundorworuld   wide dreogan.
Ne hafaþ hio blod ne ban,   hwæþre bearnum wearð
geond þisne middangeard   mongum to frofre.
20   Næfre hio heofonum hran,   ne to helle mot,
ac hio sceal wideferh   wuldorcyninges
larum lifgan.   Long is to secganne
hu hyre ealdorgesceaft   æfter gongeð,
woh wyrda gesceapu;   þæt is wrætlic þing
25   to gesecganne.   Soð is æghwylc
þara þe ymb þas wiht   wordum becneð;
ne hafað heo ænig lim,   leofaþ efne seþeah.
Gif þu mæge reselan   recene gesecgan
soþum wordum,   saga hwæt hio hatte.

Riddle Thirty-nine

Writings say a stranger lives
    among mankind much of the time,
visible and plain. It has secret power,
much more than men know.
It will visit every individual
separately, setting back out on its way.
It is never there a second night
but must forever roam homeless
on the road of exile, no more wretched for that.
It never lands on earth, has neither foot nor hand
nor even one single eye,
nor has a mouth, nor speaks with men,
nor has a mind, but writings say
it is the poorest of all creatures
born according to their kinds.
It has no soul nor life, but lays tracks
widely through this world of wonders.
It has no blood nor bones, yet has brought
comfort to many men throughout the earth.
It has never touched heaven, nor may go to hell,
but must live eternal in the teachings
of the king of glory. The long account
of its life's latter course
in fate's crooked decrees would be a curious thing
to tell. All is true
which wise words say about this creature;
it has no limbs, yet lives just the same.
If you can fathom riddles rightly
and swiftly, say what it is called.

Riddle Forty

Ece is se scyppend, se þas eorþan nu
wreðstuþum wealdeð ond þas world healdeð.
Rice is se reccend ond on ryht cyning
ealra anwalda, eorþan ond heofones,
5   healdeð ond wealdeð, swa he ymb þas utan hweorfeð.
He mec wrætlice worhte æt frymþe,
þa he þisne ymbhwyrft ærest sette,
heht mec wæccende wunian longe,
þæt ic ne slepe siþþan æfre,
10   ond mec semninga slæp ofergongeþ,
beoð eagan min ofestum betyned.
Þisne middangeard meahtig dryhten
mid his onwalde æghwær styreð;
swa ic mid waldendes worde ealne
15   þisne ymbhwyrft utan ymbclyppe.
Ic eom to þon bleað, þæt mec bealdlice mæg
gearu gongende grima abregan,
ond eofore eom æghwær cenra,
þonne he gebolgen bidsteal giefeð;
20   ne mæg mec oferswiþan segnberendra
ænig ofer eorþan, nymþe se ana god
se þisne hean heofon healdeþ ond wealdeþ.
Ic eom on stence strengre micle
þonne ricels oþþe rose sy,
25   on eorþan tyrf
wynlic weaxeð; ic eom wræstre þonne heo.
þeah þe lilie sy leof moncynne,
beorht on blostman, ic eom betre þonne heo;
swylce ic nardes stenc nyde oferswiþe   (cont.)

Riddle Forty

Eternal is the Creator, who controls the earth
and governs the world with his guiding rod.
Powerful is the ruler, and rightly king
over all earth and heaven, even as

5   he contains all those he commands and controls.
He wrought me radiantly at the origin
when he first founded this world,
ordered me to wait long ages on watch
so that since then I should never sleep,

10   but sleep comes suddenly upon me
and my eyes are quickly covered.
The mighty lord guides this middle-earth
in all places by his power;
so I by the wielder's word

15   embrace this orb in its entirety.
I am so gentle that I jump in terror
at swift-speeding shadows,
and I am bolder than the boar
bristling with rage as he stands at bay;

20   no warrior in the world
can overcome me, only God
who rules and reigns in the heights of heaven.
My fragrance is fairer by far
than that of incense or the rose,

25   in earth's turf
daintily growing; I am more delicate than her.
Though the lily is loved by men,
bright in blossom, I am better than her;
so too I always swamp the scent of nard   (cont.)

30 mid minre swetnesse symle æghwær,
ond ic fulre eom þonne þis fen swearte
þæt her yfle adelan stinceð.
Eal ic under heofones hwearfte recce,
swa me leof fæder lærde æt frymþe,
35 þæt ic þa mid ryhte reccan moste
þicce ond þynne; þinga gehwylces
onlicnesse æghwær healde.
Hyrre ic eom heofone, hateþ mec heahcyning
his deagol þing dyre bihealdan;
40 eac ic under eorþan eal sceawige
wom wraðscrafu wraþra gæsta.
Ic eom micle yldra þonne ymbhwyrft þes
oþþe þes middangeard meahte geweorþan,
ond ic giestron wæs geong acenned
45 mære to monnum þurh minre modor hrif.
Ic eom fægerre frætwum goldes,
þeah hit mon awerge wirum utan;
ic eom wyrslicre þonne þes wudu fula
oðða þis waroð þe her aworpen ligeð.
50 Ic eorþan eom æghwær brædre,
ond widgielra þonne þes wong grena;
folm mec mæg bifon ond fingras þry
utan eaþe ealle ymbclyppan.
Heardra ic eom ond caldra þonne se hearda forst,
55 hrim heorugrimma, þonne he to hrusan cymeð;
ic eom Ulcanus up irnendan
leohtan leoman lege hatra.
Ic eom on goman gena swetra
þonne þu beobread blende mid hunige;
60 swylce ic eom wraþre þonne wermod sy, (cont.)

30   with the sweetness of my perfume everywhere,
and I am fouler than this black fen
which lies here stinking in its loathsome filth.
I rule all things under heaven's range,
as the dear father taught me in the first days
35   that 1 rightly rule both
thick and thin; and thoroughly
embrace the images of all things made.
Higher I am than heaven, whose high king
commands me to behold his hidden secrets;
40   also under earth I occupy
the putrid evil pits of hostile spirits.
I am much older than this universe
or this middle-earth might yet become,
and yesterday I was young, reborn
45   from my mother's womb, a glory for mankind.
I am more gorgeous than golden ornaments,
even those men fret with filigree;
I am worse than this rotten wood
or this kelp that lies here cast away.
50   I am everywhere broader than earth
and vaster than this verdant plain;
a hand may hold me, and three fingers
easily enclose me in their clasp.
Harder I am and colder than the harsh frost,
55   the grim rime, when it grips the ground;
I am hotter than the hurtling
flames of Vulcan's flashing light.
I am sweeter still on the tongue
than bread blended with bees' honey;
60   so too I am more bitter than the wormwood   (cont.)

þe her on hyrstum   heasewe stondeþ.
Ic mesan mæg   meahtelicor
ond efnetan   ealdum þyrse,
ond ic gesælig mæg   symle lifgan
65 þeah ic ætes ne sy   æfre to feore.
Ic mæg fromlicor   fleogan þonne pernex
oþþe earn oþþe hafoc   æfre meahte;
nis zefferus,   se swifta wind,
þæt swa fromlice mæg   feran æghwær;
70 me is snægl swiftra,   snelra regnwyrm
ond fenyce   fore hreþre;
is þæs gores sunu   gonge hrædra,
þone we wifel   wordum nemnað.
Hefigere ic eom micle   þonne se hara stan
75 oþþe unlytel   leades clympre,
leohtre ic eom micle   þonne þes lytla wyrm
þe her on flode gæð   fotum dryge.
Flinte ic eom heardre   þe þis fyr drifeþ
of þissum strongan   style heardan,
80 hnescre ic eom micle   halsrefeþre,
seo her on winde   wæweð on lyfte.
Ic eorþan eom   æghwær brædre
ond widgelra   þonne þes wong grena;
ic uttor eaþe   eal ymbwinde,
85 wrætlice gewefen   wundorcræfte.
Nis under me   ænig oþer
wiht waldendre   on worldlife;
ic eom ufor   ealra gesceafta,
þara þe worhte   waldend user,
90 se mec ana mæg   ecan meahtum,
geþeon þrymme,   þæt ic onþunian ne sceal.   (cont.)

68

which grows here grey in the copse.
I can munch as mightily
and feast as fast as ancient giants,
and I can live happily forever
65   even though I never eat.
I can fly faster than pheasant
or eagle or hawk ever could;
there is no zephyr or zooming wind
that can swish so swiftly anywhere;
70   the snail outstrips me, earthworm
and fen-frog move faster;
that son of dung we call the weevil
walks with fleeter foot.
I am heavier by far than the hoary rock
75   or the dense dead mass of lead;
I am lighter by far than this little worm
which walks here on the water with dry feet.
I am harder than the flint which strikes fire
from this strong tough steel;
80   I am softer by far than downy feathers
floating here aloft in the breeze.
I am everywhere broader than earth
and vaster than this verdant plain;
From afar I embrace all with ease,
85   strangely woven with wondrous skill.
Under me there is no other
being of more authority in the world's age;
I am above all creatures
whom our ruler raised,
90   who alone can increase my powers
or tame my might, temper my pride.   (cont.)

Mara ic eom ond strengra   þonne se micla hwæl,
se þe garsecges   grund bihealdeð
sweartan syne;   ic eom swiþre þonne he,
95   swylce ic eom on mægene   minum læsse
þonne se hondwyrm,   se þe hæleþa bearn,
secgas searoþoncle,   seaxe delfað.
Nu hafu ic in heafde   hwite loccas
wræste gewundne,   ac ic eom wide calu;
100   ne ic breaga ne bruna   brucan moste,
ac mec bescyrede   scyppend eallum;
nu me wrætlice   weaxað on heafde
þæt me on gescyldrum   scinan motan
ful wrætlice   wundne loccas.
105   Mara ic eom ond fættra   þonne amæsted swin,
bearg bellende,   þe on bocwuda,
won wrotende   wynnum lifde
þæt he

Riddle Forty-one

edniwu;
þæt is moddor   monigra cynna,
þæs selestan,   þæs sweartestan,
þæs deorestan   þæs þe dryhta bearn
5   ofer foldan sceat   to gefean agen.
Ne magon we her in eorþan   owiht lifgan,
nymðe we brucen   þæs þa bearn doð.
þæt is to geþencanne   þeoda gehwylcum,
wisfæstum werum,   hwæt seo wiht sy.

I am huger and stronger than the mighty whale
who gazes on the ocean's depth
with swarthy face; my force exceeds his,
95   just as my strength is weaker
than the earthworm which the sons of
artful men dig up with knives.
I have no delicate curly locks
of blonde hair on my head, for I am bald;
100 I have no use for brows or eyelids,
but my creator cut them all away;
now growing graciously on my head
to shimmer on my shoulders
full of splendour are those other curly locks.
105 I am stouter and fatter than the mast-fed swine,
the grunting pig grubbing away
his blissful life in beech-woods
so that he . . . .

Riddle Forty-one

renewed;
it is the mother of many races,
the best the blackest
the dearest which the sons of men
upon the earth's face own in gladness.
We can not live at all here in the world
without enjoying what these infants do.
Wise men of each and every nation
must think what this creature is.

Ic seah wyhte   wrætlice twa
undearnunga   ute plegan
hæmedlaces;   hwitloc anfeng
wlanc under wædum,   gif þæs weorces speow,
5   fæmne fyllo.   Ic on flette mæg
þurh runstafas   rincum secgan,
þam þe bec witan,   bega ætsomne
naman þara wihta.   Þær sceal Nyd wesan
twega oþer   ond se torhta Æsc
10   an an linan,   Acas twegen,
Hægelas swa some.   Hwylc þæs hordgates
cægan cræfte   þa clamme onleac
þe þa rædellan   wið rynemenn
hygefæste heold   heortan bewrigene
15   orþoncbendum?   Nu is undyrne
werum æt wine   hu þa wihte mid us,
heanmode twa,   hatne sindon

Riddle Forty-two

I saw two curious creatures
brazenly splicing their flesh
in outdoor sport; if the trick worked
the haughty blonde's belly would hummock
under her skirts. On the floor I can
spell out in rune-staves
to book-wise men the names of both
beasts together. N E E D shall be there
twice and the bright A S H
once in the line, two O A K S,
H A I L twice too. Who can with key's craft
unlock the door to the hoard
which holds the riddle hard in thought
against rune-guessers, its heart covered
by cunning bonds? Now is revealed
to men at wine the names we give
to these two shameless creatures.

Riddle Forty-three

Ic wat indryhtne   æþelum deorne
giest in geardum,   þam se grimma ne mæg
hungor sceððan   ne se hata þurst,
yldo ne adle.   Gif him arlice
5   esne þenað,   se þe agan sceal
on þam siðfate,   hy gesunde æt ham
findað witode him   wiste ond blisse,
cnosles unrim,   care, gif se esne
his hlaforde   hyreð yfle,
10   frean on fore.   Ne wile forht wesan
broþor oþrum;   him þæt bam sceðeð,
þonne hy from bearme   begen hweorfað
anre magan   ellorfuse,
moddor ond sweostor.   Mon, se þe wille,
15   cyþe cynewordum   hu se cuma hatte,
eðþa se esne,   þe ic her ymb sprice.

Riddle Forty-four

Wrætlic hongað   bi weres þeo,
frean under sceate.   Foran is þyrel.
Bið stiþ ond heard,   stede hafað godne;
þonne se esne   his agen hrægl
5   ofer cneo hefeð,   wile þæt cuþe hol
mid his hangellan   heafde gretan
þæt he efenlang ær   oft gefylde.

Riddle Forty-three

I know a noble precious guest
in human dwelling, whom grim hunger
cannot harm nor hot thirst,
old age nor illness. If the attendant
who goes with him on his journey
serves him well they shall find
feasting and bliss, countless kindred awaiting them
safe at the road's end; but only sorrow
if the servant disobeys his lord
and master on their travels. Nor will one brother
fear another; eager for the journey
they will both suffer when they leave
the bosom of their one kinswoman,
their mother and sister. The man who will,
let him reveal in fit words how this guest is named,
or the servant I speak of here.

Riddle Forty-four

Strangely hangs by man's thigh
below his lap. In front is hole.
Is stiff and hard, stands in good stead
when the man his own skirt
over knee hoists, wants that known hole
with his dangler's head to greet,
fill it as he filled it long and oft before.

Riddle Forty-five

Ic on wincle gefrægn   weaxan nathwæt,
þindan ond þunian,   þecene hebban;
on þæt banlease   bryd grapode,
hygewlonc hondum,   hrægle þeahte
5   þrindende þing   þeodnes dohtor.

Riddle Forty-six

Wer sæt æt wine   mid his wifum twam
ond his twegen suno   ond his twa dohtor,
swase gesweostor,   ond hyra suno twegen,
freolico frumbearn;   fæder wæs þær inne
5   þara æþelinga   æghwæðres mid,
eam ond nefa.   Ealra wæron fife
eorla ond idesa   insittendra.

Riddle Forty-seven

Moððe word fræt.   Me þæt þuhte
wrætlicu wyrd,   þa ic þæt wundor gefrægn,
þæt se wyrm forswealg   wera gied sumes,
þeof in þystro,   þrymfæstne cwide
5   ond þæs strangan staþol.   Stælgiest ne wæs
wihte þy gleawra,   þe he þam wordum swealg.

Riddle Forty-five

In a corner I heard something growing,
  stretching and stiffening, lifting its shirt;
a proud girl grasped the boneless
thing in her hands, prince's daughter
covered the swelling thing with her apron.

Riddle Forty-six

A man sat at wine with his two wives
  and his two sons and his two daughters,
sweet sisters, and their two sons,
handsome first-born ones; the father of
each of those fine youths was in there too,
uncle and nephew. In all there were five
men and women sitting inside.

Riddle Forty-seven

A moth ate words. A marvel to me
  when I found out their strange fate,
that the worm swallowed some man's song,
a thief in the night filched his fine speech
and its stout structure. The stealing guest
was not a whit the wiser for the words he guzzled.

Riddle Forty-eight

Ic gefrægn for hæleþum   hring endean,
torhtne butan tungan,   tila þeah he hlude
stefne ne cirmde,   strongum wordum.
Sinc for secgum   swigende cwæð:
5   "Gehæle mec,   helpend gæsta."
Ryne ongietan   readan goldes
guman galdorcwide,   gleawe beþencan
hyra hælo to gode,   swa se hring gecwæð.

Riddle Forty-nine

Ic wat eardfæstne   anne standan,
deafne, dumban,   se oft dæges swilgeð
þurh gopes hond   gifrum lacum.
Hwilum on þam wicum   se wonna þegn,
5   sweart ond saloneb,   sendeð oþre
under goman him   golde dyrran,
þa æþelingas   oft wilniað,
cyningas ond cwene.   Ic þæt cyn nu gen
nemnan ne wille,   þe him to nytte swa
10   ond to dugþum doþ   þæt se dumba her,
eorp unwita,   ær forswilgeð.

Riddle Forty-eight

I heard a bright ring interceding
for men; tongueless, with no loud voice,
yet it cried out well in strong words.
The treasure spoke mutely for men:
"Save me, helper of souls."
Let men fathom the red gold's
mysteries and spell-speech, let the wise commit
their souls' salvation to God, as the ring said.

Riddle Forty-nine

I know a thing standing fixed to the ground,
deaf, dumb, who by day often swills
gifts greedily from servant's hand.
At times in rooms the dark thane,
swarthy, sallow-faced, sends others
under his gum, dearer than gold,
which kings and queens and nobles
often desire. I will not yet
name the thing which serves them so
and does them good, which the dumb
dark witless thing first swallows.

Riddle Fifty

Wiga is on eorþan   wundrum acenned
dryhtum to nytte,   of dumbum twam
torht atyhted,   þone on teon wigeð
feond his feonde.   Forstrangne oft
5   wif hine wrið;   he him wel hereð,
þeowaþ him geþwære,   gif him þegniað
mægeð ond mæcgas   mid gemete ryhte,
fedað hine fægre;   he him fremum stepeð
life on lissum.   Leanað grimme
10   þam þe hine wloncne   weorþan læteð.

Riddle Fifty-one

Ic seah wrætlice   wuhte feower
samed siþian;   swearte wæran lastas,
swaþu swiþe blacu.   Swift wæs on fore,
fuglum framra;   fleag on lyfte,
5   deaf under yþe.   Dreag unstille
winnende wiga   se him wegas tæcneþ
ofer fæted gold   feower eallum.

Riddle Fifty

He is the world's warrior, born in wonder
for mankind's good, begot by two mutes,
hatched glittering, hurled in hate
by foe against foe. Woman fetters
his strength daily; he bows in duty,
serves meekly if maids and men
attentively tend his needs,
feed him faithfully; he favours them
with life's delights. Dire his vengeance
when his pride is left unleashed.

Riddle Fifty-one

I saw four curious creatures
travelling together; their tracks were swarthy
pitch-black swathes. Moving swiftly
the birds' pivot flew aloft,
plunged under wave. The working warrior
toiled tirelessly, taught all four
their paths through precious gold.

Riddle Fifty-two

Ic seah ræpingas   in ræced fergan
under hrof sales   hearde twegen,
þa wæron genamnan,   nearwum bendum
gefeterade   fæste togædre;
5   þara oþrum wæs   an getenge
wonfah Wale,   seo weold hyra
bega siþe   bendum fæstra.

Riddle Fifty-three

Ic seah on bearwe   beam hlifian,
tanum torhtne.   þæt treow wæs on wynne,
wudu weaxende.   Wæter hine ond eorþe
feddan fægre,   oþþæt he frod dagum
5   on oþrum wearð   aglachade
deope gedolgod,   dumb in bendum,
wriþen ofer wunda,   wonnum hyrstum
foran gefrætwed.   Nu he fæcnum weg
þurh his heafdes mægen   hildegieste
10   oþrum rymeð.   Oft hy an yste strudon
hord ætgædre;   hræd wæs ond unlæt
se æftera,   gif se ærra fær
genamnan in nearowe   neþan moste.

Riddle Fifty-two

I saw roped captives, two tough comrades
fettered fast together, fetched
chained in chafing bonds
to a room under hall's roof;
close by one of them stood
the dark-haired slave who sent them
on their journey, inseparably joined.

Riddle Fifty-three

I saw tall timber stand in forest,
brightness of boughs. The tree branched
in woody rapture. Rain and soil
nourished him through numbered days
until he fell in affliction,
deeply wounded, dumb in chains,
his gashes plated, patched up
in a black hood. Now his bleak head
rives a road for some other
crafty foe. In battle's crash they
plunder hoards together. His tail
wags hard when his head must brave
danger for a comrade in distress.

Riddle Fifty-four

Hyse cwom gangan,　þær he hie wisse
stondan in wincle,　stop feorran to,
hror hægstealdmon,　hof his agen
hrægl hondum up,　hrand under gyrdels
5　hyre stondendre　stiþes nathwæt,
worhte his willan;　wagedan buta.
Þegn onnette,　wæs þragum nyt
tillic esne,　teorode hwæþre
æt stunda gehwam　strong ær þon hio,
10　werig þæs weorces.　Hyre weaxan ongon
under gyrdelse　þæt oft gode men
ferðþum freogað　ond mid feo bicgað.

Riddle Fifty-five

Ic seah in healle,　þær hæleð druncon,
on flet beran　feower cynna,
wrætlic wudutreow　ond wunden gold,
sinc searobunden,　ond seolfres dæl
5　ond rode tacn,　þæs us to roderum up
hlædre rærde,　ær he helwara
burg abræce.　Ic þæs beames mæg
eaþe for eorlum　æþelu secgan;
þær wæs hlin ond acc　ond se hearda iw
10　ond se fealwa holen;　frean sindon ealle
nyt ætgædre,　naman habbað anne,
wulfheafedtreo,　þæt oft wæpen abæd
his mondryhtne,　maðm in healle,
goldhilted sweord.　Nu me þisses gieddes
15　ondsware ywe,　se hine on mede
wordum secgan　hu se wudu hatte.

84

Riddle Fifty-four

A man came walking where he knew
she stood in a corner, stepped forward;
the bold fellow plucked up his own
skirt by hand, stuck something stiff
beneath her belt as she stood,
worked his will; they both wiggled.
The man hurried; his trusty helper
plied a handy task, but tired
at length, less strong now than she,
weary of the work. Thick beneath
her belt swelled the thing good men
praise both with their hearts and purses.

Riddle Fifty-five

In the hall where heroes drank I saw
a four-fold thing set on the floor;
a rare wood-tree; gold wired
skilfully as a gem; a silvered jewel;
and his cross-sign who raised a ladder
to heaven for us, then stormed the fort
of hell's denizens. Easy for me
to tell men this tree's nature;
there was maple and oak and hard yew
and yellow holly all together
useful to a lord, sharing one name,
wolf-head-tree, handing weapons
to its lord, treasure in the hall,
gold-hilted swords. Now send me answer
to this song, whoever dares
tell in words what this tree is called.

Riddle Fifty-six

Ic wæs þær inne   þær ic ane geseah
winnende wiht   wido bennegean,
holt hweorfende;   heaþoglemma feng,
deopra dolga.   Daroþas wæron
5   weo þære wihte,   ond se wudu searwum
fæste gebunden.   Hyre fota wæs
biidfæst oþer,   oþer bisgo dreag,
leolc on lyfte,   hwilum londe neah.
Treow wæs getenge   þam þær torhtan stod
10   leafum bihongen.   Ic lafe geseah
minum hlaforde,   þær hæleð druncon,
þara flana geweorc,   on flet beran.

Riddle Fifty-seven

Ðeos lyft byreð   lytle wihte
ofer beorghleoþa.   Þa sind blace swiþe,
swearte salopade.   Sanges rope
heapum ferað,   hlude cirmað,
5   tredað bearonæssas,   hwilum burgsalo
niþþa bearna.   Nemnað hy sylfe.

Riddle Fifty-six

Inside a house I saw
   a striving creature, stabbed by wood,
a darting slat ; it suffered battle-slashes,
gaping clefts. Arrows caused
the creature torment, as did the deft slat,
firmly tethered. One of its feet
stood still, the other plied its task,
played now aloft, now near the ground.
A tree stood close by, brightly
hung with leaves. Where heroes drank
I saw the outcome of the arrows' work
borne in the hall before my lord.

Riddle Fifty-seven

This air carries little creatures
   over hillsides. They are very bright,
black, dark-coated. Rich with song
they roam in flocks, cry loudly,
tread woody headlands, even the halls
of men. They name themselves.

Ic wat anfete   ellen dreogan
wiht on wonge.   Wide ne fereð,
ne fela rideð,   ne fleogan mæg
þurh scirne dæg,   ne hie scip fereð,
5   naca nægledbord;   nyt bið hwæþre
hyre mondryhtne   monegum tidum.
Hafað hefigne steort,   heafod lytel,
tungan lange,   toð nænigne,
isernes dæl;   eorðgræf þæþeð.
10   Wætan ne swelgeþ   ne wiht iteþ,
foþres ne gitsað,   fereð oft swa þeah
lagoflod on lyfte;   life ne gielpeð,
hlafordes gifum,   hyreð swa þeana
þeodne sinum.   Þry sind in naman
15   ryhte runstafas,   þara is Rad foran.

Riddle Fifty-eight

I know a one-footed beast, boldly
working in the field. It walks not far
nor rides much, nor can fly
through shining day; no ship's clinkered
prow takes it, yet time and again
it profits its prince.
Tail heavy, head small,
long tongue, no tooth,
partly iron, it paces an earth-grave.
Swallows no water, eats nothing,
craves no fodder, yet often ferries
water-streams aloft; alive, flaunts
no lord's gifts, but must obey
its master. In its name are three
true rune-staves, of which R is first.

Ic seah in healle   hring gyldenne
men sceawian,   modum gleawe,
ferþþum frode.   Friþospede bæd
god nergende   gæste sinum
5 se þe wende wriþan;   word æfter cwæð
hring on hyrede,   hælend nemde
tillfremmendra.   Him torhte in gemynd
his dryhtnes naman   dumba brohte
ond in eagna gesihð,   gif þæs æþelan
10 goldes tacen   ongietan cuþe
ond dryhtnes dolg,   don swa þæs beages
benne cwædon.   Ne mæg þære bene
æniges monnes   ungefullodre
godes ealdorburg   gæst gesecan,
15 rodera ceastre.   Ræde, se þe wille,
hu ðæs wrætlican   wunda cwæden
hringes to hæleþum,   þa he in healle wæs
wylted ond wended   wloncra folmum.

Riddle Fifty-nine

In a hall I saw sage-hearted
wise-minded men behold
a golden ring. He who turned the ring
prayed for peace and joy of spirit
to God the Saviour; then the ring spoke
words to the assembly, invoked the Saviour
of the righteous. The dumb ring brought
his lord's name alight in his mind
and vision when he could see
the symbol of the noble gold
and the Lord's wounds, do as the
ring's wounds said. Unfulfilled
by prayer, no man's soul
may seek God's royal city,
the heavenly dwelling. Let him who will
say how this wondrous ring's wounds
spoke to heroes when in the hall
it was turned and passed in proud men's hands.

Riddle Sixty

Ic wæs be sonde,   sæwealle neah,
æt merefaroþe,   minum gewunade
frumstaþole fæst;   fea ænig wæs
monna cynnes,   þæt minne þær
5   on anæde   eard beheolde,
ac mec uhtna gehwam   yð sio brune
lagufæðme beleolc.   Lyt ic wende
þæt ic ær oþþe sið   æfre sceolde
ofer meodubence   muðleas sprecan,
10   wordum wrixlan.   Þæt is wundres dæl,
on sefan searolic   þam þe swylc ne conn,
hu mec seaxes ord   ond seo swiþre hond,
eorles ingeþonc   ond ord somod,
þingum geþydan,   þæt ic wiþ þe sceolde
15   for unc anum twam   ærendspræce
abeodan bealdlice,   swa hit beorna ma
uncre wordcwidas   widdor ne mænden.

Riddle Sixty-one

Oft mec fæste bileac   freolicu meowle,
ides on earce,   hwilum up ateah
folmum sinum   ond frean sealde,
holdum þeodne,   swa hio haten wæs.
5   Siðþan me on hreþre   heafod sticade,
nioþan upweardne,   on nearo fegde.
Gif þæs ondfengan   ellen dohte,
mec frætwedne   fyllan sceolde
ruwes nathwæt.   Ræd hwæt ic mæne.

Riddle Sixty

By sand, by sea-wall,
  close to water-surge I dwelt,
firm on my footing; few or no
humans there beheld
my solitary home,
but every dawn the dark wave
lapped me in watery folds. Little I thought
that sooner or later I should ever
speak mouthless across the mead-bench,
utter words. A wonder and a
marvel for minds who cannot fathom
how knife-point and right hand,
man's craft and tool combined,
contrived that I could
boldly utter errand-speech
for we two alone, so no other men
could spread our words more widely.

Riddle Sixty-one

Often a lovely lady locked me
  in a chest, at times took me out
in her hands and held me for
her kind lord, as she was commanded.
Then in my heart he stuck his head,
up from below, stuffed it tight.
If my strength survived the onslaught,
some rough thing would fill
and flatter me. Guess what I mean.

Riddle Sixty-two

Ic eom heard ond scearp,   hingonges strong,
forðsiþes from,   frean unforcuð,
wade under wambe   ond me weg sylfa
ryhtne geryme.   Rinc bið on ofeste,
5   se mec on þyð   æftanweardne,
hæleð mid hrægle;   hwilum ut tyhð
of hole hatne,   hwilum eft fareð
on nearo nathwær,   nydeþ swiþe
suþerne secg.   Saga hwæt ic hatte.

Riddle Sixty-three

Oft ic secga   seledreame sceal
fægre onþeon,   þonne ic eom forð boren
glæd mid golde,   þær guman drincað.
Hwilum mec on cofan   cysseð muþe
5   tillic esne,   þær wit tu beoþ,
fæðme on folme,   fingrum þyð,
wyrceð his willa...
        fulre,   þonne ic forð cyme
......
10   Ne mæg ic þy miþan,
       siþþan on leohte
......
swylce eac bið sona
       getacnad,   hwæt me to
15   ...leas rinc,   þa unc geryde wæs.

Riddle Sixty-two

I am hard and sharp, strong to pierce,
swift to retreat, my master's slave;
I delve under belly and drill my own
straight track. The gloved man
urging me from the rear
works in haste; now he whisks me
hot from the hole, then rams me back
in some tight spot, thrusting hard,
the southron. Say what I'm called.

Riddle Sixty-three

Often I flourish fairly amid
human joys when I am fetched out,
gaudy with gold, where men drink.
Sometimes a fine servant kisses my mouth
when we two are together in a room,
fondles and fingers me,
works his will
     full, when I come forth

I can not thus conceal
     then in light

so too is straight away
   signified, what to me
  -less man, which was easy for us.

Riddle Sixty-four

Ic seah ᚹ ond ᛁ   ofer wong faran,
beran ᛒ ᛖ; bæm wæs on siþþe
hæbbendes hyht   ᚻ ond ᚠ
swylce þryþa dæl, ᚦ ond ᛖ.
5   Gefeah ᛟ ond ᚠ   fleah ofer ᛏ
ᚻ ond ᛢ   sylfes þæs folces.

Riddle Sixty-five

Cwico wæs ic, ne cwæð ic wiht,   cwele ic efne seþeah.
Ær ic wæs, eft ic cwom. Æghwa mec reafað,
hafað mec on headre,   ond min heafod scireþ,
biteð mec on bær lic,   briceð mine wisan.
5   Monnan ic ne bite,   nympþe he me bite;
sindan þara monige   þe mec bitað.

Riddle Sixty-six

Ic eom mare   þonne þes middangeard,
læsse þonne hondwyrm,   leohtre þonne mona,
swiftre þonne sunne. Sæs me sind ealle
flodas on fæðmum   ond þes foldan bearm,
5   grene wongas. Grundum ic hrine,
helle underhnige,   heofonas oferstige,
wuldres eþel,   wide ræce
ofer engla eard,   eorþan gefylle,
ealne middangeard   ond merestreamas
10   side mid me sylfum. Saga hwæt ic hatte.

Riddle Sixty-four

I saw W and I cross the field
bearing B and E; both felt happy
in holding, H and A
joined forces too, TH and E.
F and Æ rejoiced, flew over EA,
S and P, the people's own.

Riddle Sixty-five

I am alive, I say nothing, even so I kill.
Before I was, back I came. Everyone robs me,
shuts me up and shears my head,
bites my bare flesh, breaks my spine.
I bite no man, save he bites me;
many there are who bite me.

Riddle Sixty-six

I am mightier than this middle-world,
weaker than earth-worm, brighter than moon,
swifter than sun. Seas and all waters
and the earth's green-breasted fields
I hold in my arms. I fathom the deep,
I delve below hell, soar above heaven,
glory's homeland, range widely
over angels' regions, pervade the whole
world of earth and ocean streams
with my own being. Say what I am called.

Riddle Sixty-seven

Ic on þinge gefrægn   þeodcyninges
wrætlice wiht,   wordgaldra
...... snytt... hio symle deð
fira gehwam

5   wisdome.   Wundor me þæt
       nænne muð hafað
fet ne
       welan oft sacað,
cwiþeð   wearð

10   leoda lareow.   Forþon nu longe
...... ealdre   ece lifgan
missenlice,   þenden menn bugað
eorþan sceatas.   Ic þæt oft geseah
golde gegierwed,   þær guman druncon,
15   since ond seolfre.   Secge se þe cunne,
wisfæstra hwylc,   hwæt seo wiht sy.

Riddle Sixty-eight

Ic þa wiht geseah   on weg feran;
heo wæs wrætlice   wundrum gegierwed.

Riddle Sixty-nine

Wundor wearð on wege;   wæter wearð to bane.

Riddle Sixty-seven

At the king's council I heard
a strange creature, word-songs'
    wise   it always does
for all men
        wisdom. I wonder that
            has no mouth
nor feet
        fights against wealth,
says   was
peoples' teacher. So now for a long time
        live eternal life
in various ways, while men dwell
in earth's domains. I often saw it
adorned with gold, with gems and silver,
where men drank. Let any wise man say
who knows what this thing is.

Riddle Sixty-eight

I saw the creature crawl away;
it was weirdly wreathed in wonder.

Riddle Sixty-nine

Wonder formed in wave; water turned to bone.

Riddle Seventy

Wiht is wrætlic   þam þe hyre wisan ne conn.
Singeð þurh sidan.   Is se sweora woh,
orþoncum geworht;   hafaþ eaxle tua
scearp on gescyldrum.   His gesceapo dreogeð
5   þe swa wrætlice   be wege stonde
heah ond hleortorht   hæleþum to nytte.

Riddle Seventy-one

Ic eom rices æht,   reade bewæfed,
stið ond steapwong.   Staþol wæs iu þa
wyrta wlitetorhtra;   nu eom wraþra laf,
fyres ond feole,   fæste genearwad,
5   wire geweorþad.   Wepeð hwilum
for minum gripe   se þe gold wigeð,
þonne ic yþan sceal
hringum gehyrsted.   Me
                    dryhtne min...
10   wlite bete.

Riddle Seventy

A thing strange to one strange to its ways.
Sings through its side. The neck is bent,
subtly shaped; has two sharp
flanges on the shoulders. Flame-hued,
rising tall at the road's edge,
its form fits human uses.

Riddle Seventy-one

I am the strong man's asset, striped with red,
stiff, sheer and flat. I stood before
among radiant plants; now battered by foes,
by fire and file, I am firmly bound,
adorned with wire. He who wears gold
sometimes weeps at my bite
when I must destroy
decked in rings. Me
to my lord
looks improve.

Ic wæs lytel
   geaf
     þe unc gemæne
     sweostor min,
5   fedde mec ...... oft ic feower teah
swæse broþor, þara onsundran gehwylc
dægtidum me drincan sealde
þurh þyrel þearle. Ic þæh on lust,
oþþæt ic wæs yldra ond þæt an forlet
10   sweartum hyrde, siþade widdor,
mearcpaþas Walas træd, moras pæðde,
bunden under beame, beag hæfde on healse,
wean on laste weorc þrowade,
earfoða dæl. Oft mec isern scod
15   sare on sidan; ic swigade,
næfre meldade monna ængum
gif me ordstæpe egle wæron.

Riddle Seventy-two

I was little
        gave
    who us together
            my sister,
fed me   often I tugged four
sweet brothers, who one by one
by daytime gave me ample drink
through a hole. I grew up happily
until I was older and set out
with the swarthy herdsman, travelled farther,
trod Welsh border-paths, paced moors,
bound under beam, a buckle on my neck,
grief in my wake, suffered pain,
a pack of troubles. Hard iron often
jabbed my flank; I was mute,
spoke no word to any man,
though goads left me aghast.

Ic on wonge aweox,   wunode þær mec feddon
hruse ond heofonwolcn,   oþþæt me onhwyrfdon
gearum frodne,   þa me grome wurdon,
of þære gecynde   þe ic ær cwic beheold,
5   onwendan mine wisan,   wegedon mec of earde,
gedydon þæt ic sceolde   wiþ gesceape minum
on bonan willan   bugan hwilum.
Nu eom mines frean   folme bysigo...
          dæl,   gif his ellen deag,
10   oþþe æfter dome
               m ærþa   fremman,
wyrcan
mec on þeode   utan

15   ond to wrohtstæp...
          eaxle gegyrde,

ond swiora smæl,   sidan fealwe
          þonne mec heaþosigel
20   scir bescineð   ond mec
fægre feormað   ond on fyrd wigeð
cræfte on hæfte.   Cuð is wide
þæt ic þristra sum   þeofes cræfte
under brægnlocan
25   hwilum eawunga   eþelfæsten
forðweard brece,   þæt ær frið hæfde.
Feringe from,   he fus þonan
wendeð of þam wicum.   Wiga se þe mine
wisan cunne,   saga hwæt ic hatte.

Riddle Seventy-three

I grew up in the field, lived where ground
and heaven-cloud fed me, until foes
plucked me from earth in my prime,
changed me from the living thing I was,
transformed me, forced me
against my nature to be governed
for a while by a killer's will.
Now I am busy in my lord's hand,
    part, if his courage holds,
or for glory
         perform mighty deeds
work
    me in people without

and in injury
      shoulder adorned

and narrow neck, dark sides
      when the sun of battle
shines shimmering on me, and
brightly burnishes me and bears me to war
craftily by shaft. It is well known
that I, with bold comrades, with thief's cunning,
under skull
at times brazenly breach a fortress
in a land which formerly had peace.
Suddenly bold, he turns eagerly
away from the camps. Warrior who
knows my ways, say what I am called.

Riddle Seventy-four

Ic wæs fæmne geong,   feaxhar cwene,
ond ænlic rinc   on ane tid;
fleah mid fuglum   ond on flode swom,
deaf under yþe,   dead mid fiscum,
5   ond on foldan stop,   hæfde ferð cwicu.

Riddle Seventy-five

Ic swiftne geseah   on swaþe feran
ᛗ ᛏ ᚾ ᚻ.

Riddle Seventy-six

Ic ane geseah   idese sittan.

Riddle Seventy-seven

Sæ mec fedde,   sundhelm þeahte,
ond mec yþa wrugon   eorþan getenge
feþelease.   Oft ic flode ongean
muð ontynde.   Nu wile monna sum
5   min flæsc fretan,   felles ne recceð,
siþþan he me of sidan   seaxes orde
hyd arypeð,   ond mec hraþe siþþan
iteð unsodene

Riddle Seventy-four

All at one time I was a tender bride,
a grey-haired hag, a handsome man;
I flew with birds, swam the sea-flood,
dived under waves, dead among fishes;
but when I walked on earth my soul glowed.

Riddle Seventy-five

I saw fleet-foot flit the trail
D. N. U. H.

Riddle Seventy-six

I saw a woman sit alone.

Riddle Seventy-seven

Sea fed me, foam-helmet roofed
and waves cloaked me close to earth,
footless. Flood-tide I met often
with open mouth. Now some man will
eat my flesh, fleece ignored,
when with knife-point he prises
hide from side, then suddenly
eats me, uncooked.....

Riddle Seventy-eight

Oft ic flodas
    cynne   minum
ond
dyde me to mose
5   swa ic him
        ne æt ham gesæt
        flote cwealde
þurh orþonc   yþum bewrigene.

Riddle Seventy-nine

Ic eom æþelinges   æht ond willa.

Riddle Eighty

Ic eom æþelinges   eaxlgestealla,
fyrdrinces gefara,   frean minum leof,
cyninges geselda.   Cwen mec hwilum
hwitloccedu   hond on legeð,
5   eorles dohtor,   þeah hio æþelu sy.
Hæbbe me on bosme   þæt on bearwe geweox.
Hwilum ic on wloncum   wicge ride
herges on ende;   heard is min tunge.
Oft ic woðboran   wordleana sum
10 agyfe æfter giedde.   Good is min wise
ond ic sylfa salo.   Saga hwæt ic hatte.

Riddle Seventy-eight

Often I waters
           to my kin
and
had for my food
        as I to him
      not sat at home
    in sea killed
  through skill   covered by waves.

Riddle Seventy-nine

I am a prince's possession and joy.

Riddle Eighty

I am a prince's comrade-in-arms,
a warrior's friend, my lord's favourite,
a king's consort. Golden-haired
lady lets her hand lie on me,
earl's daughter, noble though she be.
My heart holds what grew in the grove.
Sometimes I ride the proud horse
on the troop's flank; my tongue is harsh.
To a singer I often give some
reward for his song. My shape is sound
and my self sallow. Say what I'm called.

Riddle Eighty-one

Ic eom byledbreost,   belcedsweora,
heafod hæbbe   ond heane steort,
eagan ond earan   ond ænne foot,
hrycg ond heardnebb,   hneccan steapne
5   ond sidan twa,   sagol on middum,
eard ofer ældum.   Aglac dreoge,
þær mec wegeð   se þe wudu hrereð,
ond mec stondende   streamas beatað,
hægl se hearda,   ond hrim þeceð,
10   ond forst hreoseð,   ond fealleð snaw
on þyrelwombne,   ond ic
       wonsceaft mine.

Riddle Eighty-two

Wiht is
gongende,   greate swilgeð,
......
fell ne flæsc,   fotum gong...
5

sceal mæla gehwam

Riddle Eighty-one

I am bulge-breasted, belch-throated,
  have head and high tail,
eyes and ears and one foot,
back and sharp beak, sheer neck
and two sides, a stick in the stomach,
a perch above people. I suffer pain
when what shakes forests shifts me,
and storms beat me as I stand,
and the hard hail, and rime cloaks me,
and frost settles, and snow falls
on me with my pierced belly, and I
                    my misery.

Riddle Eighty-two

Thing is
        going, swallows earth,   .

    skin nor flesh, going afoot

shall every time.....

Frod wæs min fromcynn
biden in burgum,   siþþan bæle wearð
...... wera   lige bewunden,
fyre gefælsad.   Nu me fah warað
5   eorþan broþor,   se me ærest wearð
gumena to gyrne.   Ic ful gearwe gemon
hwa min fromcynn   fruman agette
eall of earde;   ic him yfle ne mot,
ac ic hæftnyd   hwilum arære
10   wide geond wongas.   Hæbbe ic wundra fela,
middangeardes   mægen unlytel,
ac ic miþan sceal   monna gehwylcum
degolfulne dom   dyran cræftes,
siðfæt minne.   Saga hwæt ic hatte.

Riddle Eighty-three

Ancient my ancestry
          lived in towns since I was first
swaddled in fire, scoured by flame,
men's   Now earth's enemy
and brother pens me, who was the prime
cause of my grief, who wrecked
all my roots in earth, my ancestry;
the memory returns; I can not harm him,
but all over earth, again and again
I fasten bonds. Not few my marvels,
not small my might in this world,
but I must hide my traces
from all men, my secret strength
and supreme power. Say what I am called.

An wiht is on eorþan   wundrum acenned,
hreoh ond reþe,   hafað ryne strongne,
grimme grymetað   ond be grunde fareð.
Modor is monigra   mærra wihta,
5   fæger ferende   fundað æfre;
ríeol is nearograp.   Nænig oþrum mæg
wlite ond wisan   wordum gecyþan,
hu mislic biþ   mægen þara cynna,
fyrn forðgesceaft;   fæder ealle bewat
10   or ond ende,   swylce an sunu,
mære meotudes bearn,   þurh
ond þæt hyhste mæge   halges gæstes.
       dyre cræft...

......

15   hy aweorp...
    ænig þara
       æfter ne mæg
          oþer cynn   eorþan
          þon ær wæs
20   wlitig ond wynsum,
Biþ sio moddor   mægené eacen,
wundrum bewreþed,   wistum gehladen,
hordum gehroden,   hæleþum dyre.
Mægen bið gemiclad,   meaht gesweotlad,
25   wlite biþ geweorþad   wuldornyttingum,
wynsum wuldorgimm   wloncum getenge,
clængeorn bið ond cystig,   cræfte eacen.   (cont.)

Riddle Eighty-four

A cruel, fierce creature lives on earth,
   her birth a miracle, her motion strong,
she roars savagely and sweeps the ground.
She is the mother of many mighty things,
5   running serenely, ever restless,
deep embracing. Her beauty and nature
no man can express in words,
nor count her kindred's myriad strength,
her ancient ancestry; all this her father watched,
10   her origin and end, as for a son,
creation's famous child, through...
and the holy spirit's highest power
               precious skill

15   they cast down
      any of them
         can not after
         other kin earth's
           which formerly was
20   fair and beautiful
The mother gains in strength,
stupendously nourished, stuffed with food,
adorned with treasure, dear to heroes.
Her power grows, her strength appears,
25   her beauty is honoured by the favours
of the world's glorious gem, striving for grace
and purity among the clouds, uniquely endowed.   (cont.)

Hio biþ eadgum leof,　earmum getæse,
freolic, sellic;　fromast ond swiþost,
30　gifrost ond grædgost　grundbedd trideþ,
þæs þe under lyfte　aloden wurde
ond ælda bearn　eagum sawe,
swa þæt wuldor wifeð,　worldbearna mæge,
þeah þe ferþum gleaw　gefrigen hæbbe
35　mon mode snottor　mengo wundra.
Hrusan bið heardra,　hæleþum frodra,
geofum bið gearora,　gimmum deorra;
worulde wlitigað,　wæstmum tydreð,
firene dwæsceð,
40　oft utan beweorpeð　anre þecene,
wundrum gewlitegad,　geond werþeode,
þæt wafiað　weras ofer eorþan,
þæt magon micle
Biþ stanum bestreþed,　stormum
45　　　　...timbred weall,
þrym...
hrusan hrineð,
　　　getenge,
oft searwum biþ
50　　　deaðe ne feleð,
þeah þe
　　　hreren,　hrif wundigen,

Hordword onhlid,　hæleþum
55　...wreoh,　wordum geopena,
hu mislic sy　mægen þara cynna.

To the rich precious, priceless to the poor,
supreme, superb; of all things spawned
30   under sky which the sons of men
have seen, she walks earth
boldest and strongest, keenest and greediest,
mother of world's children weaving glory -
however wise in heart a man may be,
35   however many wonders he has witnessed.
She is harder than earth, older than heroes,
greater than gifts, dearer than jewels,
beautifies the world, teems with life,
cleanses crimes,
40   often surrounds the entire nation
with a supremely lovely mantle;
men upon earth marvel at her,
great may it
She is banked with stones, by storms
45   timbered wall,
strength
touches earth
                           close
is often skilfully
50   does not feel death,
although
            shaken, they wound the belly,

Open the word-hoard, to men
55   cover, reveal in words
how myriad is the might of her race.

Riddle Eighty-five

Nis min sele swige,   ne ic sylfa hlud
ymb ...... unc dryhten scop
siþ ætsomne.   Ic eom swiftre þonne he,
þragum strengra,   he þreohtigra.
5   Hwilum ic me reste;   he sceal yrnan forð.
Ic him in wunige   a þenden ic lifge;
gif wit unc gedælað,   me bið dead witod.

Riddle Eighty-six

Wiht cwom gongan   þær weras sæton
monige on mæðle,   mode snottre;
hæfde an eage   ond earan twa,
ond *II* fet,   *XII* hund heafda,
5   hrycg ond wombe   ond honda twa,
earmas ond eaxle,   anne sweoran
ond sidan twa.   Saga hwæt ic hatte.

Riddle Eighty-seven

Ic seah wundorlice wiht;   wombe hæfde micle,
þryþum geþrungne.   Þegn folgade
mægenstrong ond mundrof;   micel me þuhte
godlic gumrinc,   grap on sona
5   heofones toþe
bleowe on eage;   hio borcade,
wancode willum.   Hio wolde seþeah
niol...

Riddle Eighty-five

My home is not hushed, nor myself loud
about   the Lord forged together
our twin fates' course. I am faster than he,
stronger sometimes, he lasts longer.
While I rest, he must run on.
I dwell in him as long as I live;
if we divide, death is my lot.

Riddle Eighty-six

A creature walked among wise men
sitting in crowded assembly;
it had one eye and two ears
and two feet and twelve hundred heads,
back and belly and two hands
arms and shoulders, one neck
and two sides. Say what I'm called.

Riddle Eighty-seven

I saw a strange thing, had a stout belly
hugely swollen. A servant stood by,
strong-muscled, tough-handed, a man
of might, who seized it suddenly,
blew through its eye
with the tooth of heaven; it barked,
wobbled with a will, yet wanted
low.....

Ic weox þær ic
ond sumor
    wæs min
  ......
5   stod ic on staðol...
      geong, swa
      seþeana
oft geond ofgeaf,
ac ic uplong stod, þær ic ......
10   ond min broþor; begen wæron hearde.
Eard wæs þy weorðra þe wit on stodan,
hyrstum þy hyrra. Ful oft unc holt wrugon,
wudubeama helm wonnum nihtum,
scildon wið scurum; unc gescop meotud.
15   Nu unc mæran twam magas uncre
sculon æfter cuman, eard oðþringan
gingran broþor. Eom ic gumcynnes
anga ofer eorþan; is min agen bæc
wonn ond wundorlic. Ic on wuda stonde
20   bordes on ende. Nis min broþor her,
ac ic sceal broþorleas bordes on ende
staþol weardian, stondan fæste;
ne wat hwær min broþor on wera æhtum
eorþan sceata eardian sceal,
25   se me ær be healfe heah eardade.
Wit wæron gesome sæcce to fremmanne;
næfre uncer awþer his ellen cyðde,
swa wit þære beadwe begen ne onþungan.
Nu mec unsceafta innan slitað,
30   wyrdaþ mec be wombe; ic gewendan ne mæg.
Æt þam spore findeð sped se þe seceð
      sawle rædes.

Riddle Eighty-eight

I grew where I
      and summer
         was my

I stood in place
      young, so
         however
often through   gave,
but I stood upright, where I...
and my brother; both were hard.
The ground we stood on grew lovelier,
more radiant by our array. Forest hid us,
timbers' helm in the dark of night
shielded us from showers; the Creator shaped us.
Now our two fine kinsmen shall
succeed us, younger brothers
seize our land. I am unique
among my kind on earth; my own back is
dark and marvellous. I stand on wood
at table's end. My brother is not here,
but I must hold my stance brotherless
at table's end, stand firm:
I do not know where in earth's expanse,
in men's domains, my brother dwells,
who once reared high beside me.
We were joined to do battle;
neither of us ever showed his mettle
without both conquering in combat.
Now monsters wound me within,
 stab my stomach; I can not revert.
Whoever seeks success will find it in their spoor
      of the soul's counsel.

Riddle Eighty-nine

se wiht,
wombe hæfde
    leþre wæs
    ...on hindan.
5   Grette
    listum worhte,
hwilum eft
þygan,   him þoncade,
siþþan
10 swæsendum swylce þrage.

Riddle Ninety

Mirum videtur mihi,
lupus ab agno tenetur;
obcubuit agnus rupi
et capit viscera lupi.
5   Dum starem et mirarem,
vidi gloriam magnam
dui lupi stantes et tertium tribulantes;
IIII pedes habebant, cum septem oculis videbant.

Riddle Eighty-nine

the thing
had a belly
was leather
behind.
Greeted
made with skill,
at times again
pressed, thanked him,
then
for food, at such a time.

Riddle Ninety

A strange thing it seemed to me,
a wolf captured by a lamb;
the lamb lay down by a rock
and pulls out the wolf's bowels.
While I stood and wondered
I saw a great marvel,
two wolves standing tormenting a third;
they had four feet, they saw with seven eyes.

Riddle Ninety-one

Min heafod is   homere geþuren,
searopila wund,   sworfen feole.
Oft ic begine   þæt me ongean sticað,
þonne ic hnitan sceal,   hringum gyrded,
5   hearde wið heardum,   hindan þyrel,
forð ascufan   þæt mines frean
mod ᛘ freoþað   middelnihtum.
Hwilum ic under bæc   bregde nebbe,
hyrde þæs hordes,   þonne min hlaford wile
10   lafe þicgan   þara þe he of life het
wælcræfte awrecan   willum sinum.

Riddle Ninety two

Ic wæs brunra beot,   beam on holte,
freolic feorhbora   ond foldan wæstm,
weres wynnstaþol   ond wifes sond,
gold on geardum.   Nu eom guðwigan
5   hyhtlic hildewæpen,   hringe
        byreð,
oþrum

Riddle Ninety-one

My head is forged by hammers,
 wounded by sly arrows, smoothed by files.
Often I swallow what sticks against me
when, girded with rings, I butt
the hole from behind, hard against hard,
shove forward what protects
my lord's heart's delight at midnight.
With my beak I draw back
the hoard's warder, when my lord wants
to take the legacies of men whose life
he drove out by slaughter, at his will.

Riddle Ninety two

I was the pride of pigs, a forest tree,
 a noble nourisher and the fruit of earth,
stock of man's delight and woman's message,
gold in courts. Now I am warrior's
trusty battle-arm, ring
            bears,
others

Frea min
　　willum sinum,
heah ond hyht...
scearpne,　hwilum
5　　　　hwilum sohte
frea...　　wod,
dægrime frod,　deope streamas,
hwilum stealc hliþo　stigan sceolde
up in eþel,　hwilum eft gewat
10　in deop dalu　duguþe secan
strong on stæpe,　stanwongas grof
hrimighearde,　hwilum hara scoc
forst of feaxe.　Ic on fusum rad
oþþæt him þone gleawstol　gingra broþor
15　min agnade　ond mec of earde adraf.
Siþþan mec isern　innanweardne
brun bennade;　blod ut ne com,
heolfor of hreþre,　þeah mec heard bite
stiðecg style.　No ic þa stunde bemearn,
20　ne for wunde weop,　ne wrecan meahte
on wigan feore　wonnsceaft mine,　　(cont.)

Riddle Ninety-three

M y lord
                 by his will
high and hope
          sharp, sometimes...
          sometimes sought
lord   waded,
old in his days, deep streams,
had sometimes to climb steep slopes
up in his own terrain, sometimes turned back
to deep valleys, seeking safety,
his step strong, he dug stony pastures
hardened by rime, hoar frost
shook from his hair. I rode the agile one
until my younger brother claimed the seat of wisdom
for himself and drove me from my dwelling.
Then bright iron wounded me
within; no blood came out,
no gore from my heart, though strong-edged steel
cut me cruelly. I neither cried then
nor wept for my wound, nor could avenge
my misery on the warrior's life,   (cont.)

ac ic aglæca ealle þolige,
þætte bord biton.   Nu ic blace swelge
wuda ond wætre,   wombe befæðme
25 þæt mec on fealleð   ufan þær ic stonde,
eorpes nathwæt;   hæbbe anne fot.
Nu min hord warað   hiþende feond,
se þe ær wide bær   wulfes gehleþan;
oft me of wombe   bewaden fereð,
30 steppeð on stið bord,
deaþes   þonne dægcondel,
sunne
        weorc   eagum wliteð
ond

but I suffered all such torments
as shields endure. Now I swallow black
wood and black water, my belly enfolds
what falls down on me where I stand,
some dark substance; I have a single foot.
Now a raiding enemy, who once carried the wolf's
comrade widely, owns my treasure;
emerging from my belly he often
steps on stiff board...
      of death   when day's candle,
sun
      act looks with eyes
and

Riddle Ninety-four

Smeþre
hyrre þonne heofon...
    glædre þonne sunne,
    ...style,
5   smeare þonne sealt
leofre þonne þis leoht eall, leohtre þon

Riddle Ninety-five

Ic eom indryhten ond eorlum cuð,
ond reste oft; ricum ond heanum,
folcum gefræge. Fere wide,
ond me fremdes ær freondum stondeð
5   hiþendra hyht, gif ic habban sceal
blæd in burgum oþþe beorhte god.
Nu snottre men swiþast lufiaþ
midwist mine; ic monigum sceal
wisdom cyþan; no þær word sprecan
10   ænig ofer eorðan. Þeah nu ælda bearn
londbuendra lastas mine
swiþe secað, ic swaþe hwilum
mine bemiþe monna gehwylcum.

Riddle Ninety-four

S moother
  higher than heaven
        gladder than sun,
            steel,
subtler than salt
lovelier than all this light, lighter than

Riddle Ninety-five

I am noble and known to men,
  and rest often among high and low,
famed among people. I travel widely,
once foreign to friends, and on me stands
robbers' joy, if I am to have
glory in towns or shining wealth.
Now wise men dearly love
my company; I shall reveal
wisdom to many, without speaking words
there upon earth. Although the sons of men
living on land now eagerly seek out
my paths, I sometimes hide
my track from everyone.

Solutions

Solutions

1. Storm, the garments etc.: leaves.
2. Storm.
3. Storm, (the first three might be read as a single riddle).
4. Bell.
5. Shield.
6. Sun.
7. Swan.
8. Nightingale.
9. Cuckoo.
10. Barnacle Goose, thought to be hatched underwater from a shell attached to timber.
11. Wine.
12. Ox.
13. Ten chickens (the skins: the inner membrane of the shell which is the chick's hall).
14. Horn.
15. Badger or fox.
16. Anchor.
17. Ballista.
18. Amphora?
19. Armed rider with hawk.
20. Sword.
21. Plough.
22. The month of December?

    Sixty riders are the sixty halfdays of the month, eleven of them being the seven holy days, plus four Sundays. The other bank on which the wagon lands is the New Year.

    Or Circling Stars? The wagon is Charles's Wain (Ursa Major) which travels daily around the Pole Star from horizon to horizon across the 'ocean' of the sky. Riders and horses are the stars near to the Wain, eleven of then, being the visible stars of the constellation Canes Venatici.

23. Bow. AGOF backwards = Foga, a mistaken or intentionally misleading spelling of *boga* 'bow'.
24. Jay, the reshuffled runes spell HIGORÆ 'jay'.
25. Onion.
26. Bible.
27. Mead.
28. Harp?
29. Moon and Sun.
30. Tree, wood.
31. Bagpipe.
32. Ship.
33. Iceberg.
34. Rake.
35. Mailcoat.
36. Ship: four feet = four oars; eight feet = four rowers in the ship; two wings = sail(s); six heads = four sailors and two figureheads of the ship.
37. Bellows.
38. Ox.
39. Day or speech.
40. Creation.
41. Water?
42. Cock & Hen. Need, Ash, Oak and Hail are the names of the runes for N, Æ, A, H respectively. The riddle thus provides N N Æ A A H H. Rearranged, these spell *hana* 'cock' and *hæn* 'hen'.
43. Body & Soul. Their mother and sister is Earth.
44. Key.
45. Dough.
46. Lot's family (see Genesis 19).
47. Bookworm.
48. Chalice.
49. Bookcase?
50. Fire.
51. Pen and fingers.

52. Two well-buckets.

53. Battering ram.

54. Churn.

55. Sword-rack? The ambiguities derive from the wooden object's likeness to a cross and a gallows. 'Wolf-head' means outlaw; 'wolf-head tree' means gallows.

56. Loom. The wood and slat are the shuttle, which 'stabs' the warp, which 'strives' as the threads move back and forth between each other. The feet are the weighted lower ends of the warp threads, one row of which remains still while the other rises and falls in the process of reversing the shed through which the shuttle passes. The 'tree' may be a distaff pole, its 'leaves' the spun wool.

57. Swallows or gnats.

58. Well-beam. A beam mounted on an upright, one end carrying a pole or rope ('long tongue') to which the bucket is attached, the other weighted to help raise the bucket. R is the first letter of the solution, probably *rod* 'pole'.

59. Chalice.

60. Reed pipe, reed pen or rune-staff.

61. Helmet.

62. Poker.

63. Beaker.

64. Hunter. Each pair of runes is the beginning of a word. A likely reading is: *WIcg* 'horse'; *BEorn* 'man'; *HAfoc* 'hawk'; *THEgn* 'servant'; *FÆlca* 'falcon'; *EA* 'water'; *SPere* 'spear'.

65. Onion.

66. Creation.

67. Bible.

68. ?

69. Ice. 68 and 69 could be read as a unit, with the solution Iceberg.

70. Pipe.

71. Sword.

72. Ox.

73. Spear.

74. Ship's figurehead?

75. Dog. DNUH is *hund* 'dog' backwards.

76. ?

77. Oyster.

78. Lamprey.

79. ? an alternative opening to 80?

80. Horn. 'What grew in grove' is mead.

81. Weathercock.

82. Harrow?

83. Ore – gold.

84. Water.

85. Fish and river.

86. One-eyed seller of garlic.

87. Bellows. 'The tooth of heaven' is wind.

88. Antler or inkhorn. 'Monsters' are quills.

89. ?

90. ?

91. Key.

92. Beech or book. Old English *boc* has both meanings.

93. Antler or inkhorn. 'Raiding enemy' is quill; 'wolf's comrade' is raven.

94. Creation.

95. Book.

Some other titles from Anglo-Saxon Books

An Introduction to the Old English Language and its Literature
Stephen Pollington

The purpose of this general introduction to Old English is not to deal with the teaching of Old English but to dispel some misconceptions about the language and to give an outline of its structure and its literature. Some basic knowledge about the origins of the English language and its early literature is essential to an understanding of the early period of English history and the present form of the language. This revised and expanded edition provides a useful guide for those contemplating embarking on a linguistic journey.

£4.95   A5   ISBN 1–898281–06–8   64 pages

First Steps in Old English
An easy to follow language course for the beginner
Stephen Pollington

A complete and easy to use Old English language course that contains all the exercises and texts needed to learn Old English. This course has been designed to be of help to a wide range of students, from those who are teaching themselves at home, to undergraduates who are learning Old English as part of their English degree course. The author has adopted a step-by-step approach that enables students of differing abilities to advance at their own pace. The course includes practice and translation exercises, a glossary of the words used in the course, and many Old English texts, including the *Battle of Brunanburh* and *Battle of Maldon*.

£16-95   ISBN 1-898281-45-9   248 x 173mm   / 10 x 6½ inches   Hardback   272 pages

Listen & Learn Old English - CD
readings of Poems, Prose and Lessons by Stephen Pollington

This CD contains lessons and texts from *First Steps in Old English*.
Tracks include: 1. Deor. 2. Beowulf – The Funeral of Scyld Scefing. 3. Engla Tocyme (The Arrival of the English). 4. Ines Domas. Two Extracts from the Laws of King Ine. 5. Deniga Hergung (The Danes' Harrying) Anglo-Saxon Chronicle Entry AD997. 6. Durham 7. The Ordeal (Be ðon ðe ordales weddigaþ) 8. Wið Dweorh (Against a Dwarf) 9. Wið Wennum (Against Wens) 10. Wið Wæterælfadle (Against Waterelf Sickness) 11. The Nine Herbs Charm 12. Læcedomas (Leechdoms) 13. Beowulf's Greeting 14. The Battle of Brunanburh 15. Blacmon – by Adrian Pilgrim. 16. A Guide to Pronunciation. 17. More than 30 other extracts of Old English verse and prose.

£9.95   ISBN 1–898281–46-7   CD - Free Old English transcript from www.asbooks.co.uk.

Wordcraft   Concise English/Old English Dictionary and Thesaurus
Stephen Pollington

Wordcraft provides Old English equivalents to the commoner modern words in both dictionary and thesaurus formats. The Thesaurus presents vocabulary relevant to a wide range of individual topics in alphabetical lists, thus making it easily accessible to those with specific areas of interest. Each thematic listing is encoded for cross-reference from the Dictionary.

The two sections will be of invaluable assistance to students of the language, as well as those with either a general or a specific interest in the Anglo-Saxon period.

£9.95   ISBN 1–898281–02–5   A5   256 pages

Leechcraft: Early English Charms, Plantlore and Healing
Stephen Pollington

An unequalled examination of every aspect of early English healing, including the use of plants, amulets, charms, and prayer. Other topics covered include Anglo-Saxon witchcraft; tree-lore; gods, elves and dwarves.

The author has brought together a wide range of evidence for the English healing tradition, and presented it in a clear and readable manner. The extensive 2,000-entry index makes it possible for the reader to quickly find specific information.

The three key Old English texts are reproduced in full, accompanied by new translations. *Bald's Third Leechbook; Lacnunga; Old English Herbarium.*

£35 ISBN 1–898281–23–8 10" x 6¾" (254 x 170mm) hardback 28 illustrations 544 pages

A Guide to Late Anglo-Saxon England
From Alfred to Eadgar II 871–1074
Donald Henson

This guide has been prepared with the aim of providing the general readers with both an overview of the period and a wealth of background information. Facts and figures are presented in a way that makes this a useful reference handbook.

Contents include: The Origins of England; Physical Geography; Human Geography; English Society; Government and Politics; The Church; Language and Literature; Personal Names; Effects of the Norman Conquest. All of the kings from Alfred to Eadgar II are dealt with separately and there is a chronicle of events for each of their reigns. There are also maps, family trees and extensive appendices.

£9.95 ISBN 1–898281–21–1 9½" x 6¾"/245 x 170mm, 6 maps & 3 family trees 208 pages

The English Elite in 1066 - Gone but not forgotten
Donald Henson

The people listed in this book formed the topmost section of the ruling elite in 1066. It includes all those who held office between the death of Eadward III (January 1066) and the abdication of Eadgar II (December 1066). There are 455 individuals in the main entries and these have been divided according to their office or position.

The following information is listed where available:

- What is known of their life;
- Their landed wealth;
- The early sources in which information about the individual can be found
- Modern references that give details about his or her life.

In addition to the biographical details, there is a wealth of background information about English society and government. A series of appendices provide detailed information about particular topics or groups of people.

£16.95 ISBN 1–898281–26–2 10 x 7 inches (250 x 175mm) 272 pages

An Introduction to Early English Law
Bill Griffiths

Much of Anglo-Saxon life followed a traditional pattern, of custom, and of dependence on kin-groups for land, support and security. The Viking incursions of the ninth century and the re-conquest of the north that followed both disturbed this pattern and led to a new emphasis on centralised power and law, with royal and ecclesiastical officials prominent as arbitrators and settlers of disputes.

The diversity and development of early English law is sampled here by selecting several law-codes to be read in translation – that of Ethelbert of Kent, being the first to be issued in England, Alfred the Great's, the most clearly thought-out of all, and short codes from the reigns of Edmund and Ethelred the Unready.

£4.95   ISBN 1–898281–14–9   A5   96 pages

Peace-Weavers and Shield-Maidens: Women in Early English Society
Kathleen Herbert

The recorded history of the English people did not start in 1066 as popularly believed but one thousand years earlier. The Roman historian Cornelius Tacitus noted in *Germania*, published in the year 98, that the English (Latin *Anglii*), who lived in the southern part of the Jutland peninsula, were members of an alliance of Goddess-worshippers. The author has taken that as an appropriate opening to an account of the earliest Englishwomen, the part they played in the making of England, what they did in peace and war, the impressions they left in Britain and on the continent, how they were recorded in the chronicles, how they come alive in heroic verse and jokes.

£4.95   ISBN 1–898281–11–4   A5   64 pages

Dark Age Naval Power
A Reassessment of Frankish and Anglo-Saxon Seafaring Activity
John Haywood

In the first edition of this work, published in 1991, John Haywood argued that the capabilities of the pre-Viking Germanic seafarers had been greatly underestimated. Since that time, his reassessment of Frankish and Anglo-Saxon shipbuilding and seafaring has been widely praised and accepted.

'The book remains a historical study of the first order. It is required reading for our seminar on medieval seafaring at Texas A & M University and is essential reading for anyone interested in the subject.'
F. H. Van Doorninck, *The American Neptune* (1994)

'The author has done a fine job, and his clear and strongly put theories will hopefully further the discussion of this important part of European history.'
Arne Emil Christensen, *The International Journal of Nautical Archaeology* (1992)

In this second edition, some sections of the book have been revised and updated to include information gained from excavations and sea trials with sailing replicas of early ships. The new evidence supports the author's argument that early Germanic shipbuilding and seafaring skills were far more advanced than previously thought. It also supports the view that Viking ships and seaborne activities were not as revolutionary as is commonly believed.

5 maps & 18 illustrations

£16.95   ISBN 1–898281–43-2   approx. 10" x 7" (245 x 170mm)   Hardback   224 pages

Anglo-Saxon Attitudes – A short introduction to Anglo-Saxonism
J.A. Hilton

This is not a book about the Anglo-Saxons, but a book about books about Anglo-Saxons. It describes the academic discipline of Anglo-Saxonism; the methods of study used; the underlying assumptions; and the uses to which it has been put.

Methods and motives have changed over time but right from the start there have been constant themes: English patriotism and English freedom.

£9.95   A5   ISBN 1–898281–39–4   Hardback   64 pages

The Origins of the Anglo-Saxons
Donald Henson

This book has come about through a growing frustration with scholarly analysis and debate about the beginnings of Anglo-Saxon England. Much of what has been written is excellent, yet unsatisfactory. One reason for this is that scholars often have only a vague acquaintance with fields outside their own specialism. The result is a partial examination of the evidence and an incomplete understanding or explanation of the period.

The growth and increasing dominance of archaeological evidence for the period has been accompanied by an unhealthy enthusiasm for models of social change imported from prehistory. Put simply, many archaeologists have developed a complete unwillingness to consider movements of population as a factor in social, economic or political change. All change becomes a result of indigenous development, and all historically recorded migrations become merely the movement of a few hundred aristocrats or soldiers. The author does not find this credible.

"This book has three great strengths . . .

First, it pulls together and summarises the whole range of evidence bearing on the subject, offering an up-to-date assessment: the book is, in other words, a highly efficient introduction to the subject. Second – perhaps reflecting Henson's position as a leading practitioner of public archaeology (he is currently Education and Outreach Co-ordinator for the Council for British Archaeology) – the book is refreshingly jargon free and accessible. Third, Henson is not afraid to offer strong, controversial interpretations. The Origins of the Anglo-Saxons can therefore be strongly recommended to those who want a detailed road-map of the evidence and debates for the migration period."

Current Archaeology

£16.95   ISBN 1–898281–40–2   9 ¾ x 6 ¾ inches   245 x 170mm   Hardback   304 pages

A Departed Music – Readings in Old English Poetry
Walter Nash

The *readings* of this book take the form of passages of translation from some Old English poems. The author paraphrases their content and discuses their place and significance in the history of poetic art in Old English society and culture.

The author's knowledge, enthusiasm and love of his subject help make this an excellent introduction to the subject for students and the general reader.

£16.95   ISBN 1–898281–37–8   9 ¾ x 6 ¾ inches   245 x 170mm   Hardback   240 pages

Rudiments of Runelore

Stephen Pollington

The purpose of this book is to provide both a comprehensive introduction for those coming to the subject for the first time, and a handy and inexpensive reference work for those with some knowledge of the subject. The *Abecedarium Nordmannicum* and the English, Norwegian and Icelandic rune poems are included as are two rune riddles, extracts from the Cynewulf poems and new work on the three Brandon runic inscriptions and the Norfolk 'Tiw' runes.

Headings include: The Origin of the Runes; Runes among the Germans; The Germanic Rune Row and the Common Germanic Language; The English Runic Tradition; The Scandinavian Runic Tradition; Runes and Pseudo-runes; The Use of Runes; Bind Runes and Runic Cryptography.

£4.95   ISBN 1–898281–16–5   A5   Illustrations   96 pages

Rune Cards

Brian Partridge & Tony Linsell

"This boxed set of 30 cards contains some of the most beautiful and descriptive black and white line drawings that I have ever seen on this subject."

Pagan News

30 pen and ink drawings by Brian Partridge
80 page booklet by Tony Linsell gives information about the origin of runes, their meaning, and how to read them.

£9.95   ISBN 1-898281-34-3   30 cards & 80 page booklet – boxed

English Sea Power 871-1100AD

John Pullen-Appleby

This work examines the largely untold story of English sea power prior to the Norman Conquest. The author illuminates the much-neglected period 871 to 1100, an age when English rulers deployed naval resources, first against Norse Invaders, and later as an instrument of state in relations with neighbouring countries.

The author has gathered together information about the crewing, appearance and use of fighting ships during the period.

£14.95   ISBN 1-898281-31-9   9 ¾ x 6 ¾ inches   245 x 170mm   128 pages

Ordering

Payment may be made by Visa, or Mastercard. Telephone orders accepted.
See website for postal address
UK deliveries add 10% up to a maximum of £2-50
Europe – including **Republic of Ireland** - add 10% plus £1 – all orders sent airmail
North America add 10% surface delivery, 30% airmail
Elsewhere add 10% surface delivery, 40% airmail
Overseas surface delivery 5–8 weeks; airmail 5–10 days
For details of other titles and our North American distributor see our website or contact us at:

Anglo-Saxon Books

www.asbooks.co.uk   Tel: 0845 430 4200

Organisations

Þa Engliscan Gesiðas

Þa Engliscan Gesiðas (The English Companions) is a historical and cultural society exclusively devoted to Anglo-Saxon history. Its aims are to bridge the gap between scholars and non-experts, and to bring together all those with an interest in the Anglo-Saxon period, its language, culture and traditions, so as to promote a wider interest in, and knowledge of all things Anglo-Saxon. The Fellowship publishes a journal, *Wiðowinde,* which helps members to keep in touch with current thinking on topics from art and archaeology to heathenism and Early English Christianity. The Fellowship enables like-minded people to keep in contact by publicising conferences, courses and meetings that might be of interest to its members.

For further details see www.tha-engliscan-gesithas.org.uk or write to:
Membership Secretary, Þa Engliscan Gesiðas, BM Box 4336, London, WC1N 3XX England.

Regia Anglorum

Regia Anglorum was founded to accurately re-create the life of the British people as it was around the time of the Norman Conquest. Our work has a strong educational slant. We consider authenticity to be of prime importance and prefer, where possible, to work from archaeological materials. Approximately twenty-five per cent of our members, of over 500 people, are archaeologists or historians.

The Society has a large working Living History Exhibit, teaching and exhibiting more than twenty crafts in an authentic environment. We own a forty-foot wooden ship replica of a type that would have been a common sight in Northern European waters around the turn of the first millennium AD. Battle re-enactment is another aspect of our activities, often involving 200 or more warriors.

For further information see www.regia.org or contact:
K. J. Siddorn, 9 Durleigh Close, Headley Park, Bristol BS13 7NQ, England

The Sutton Hoo Society

Our aims and objectives focus on promoting research and education relating to the Anglo Saxon Royal cemetery at Sutton Hoo, Suffolk in the UK. The Society publishes a newsletter SAXON twice a year, which keeps members up to date with society activities, carries resumes of lectures and visits, and reports progress on research and publication associated with the site. If you would like information about membership see website: www.suttonhoo.org

Wuffing Education

Wuffing Education provides those interested in the history, archaeology, literature and culture of the Anglo-Saxons with the chance to meet experts and fellow enthusiasts for a whole day of in-depth seminars and discussions. Day Schools take place at the historic Tranmer House overlooking the burial mounds of Sutton Hoo in Suffolk.

For details of programme of events contact:-
Wuffing Education, 4 Hilly Fields, Woodbridge, Suffolk IP12 4DX
email education@wuffings.co.uk   website www.wuffings.co.uk
Tel. 01394 383908 or 01728 688749

Places to visit

Bede's World at Jarrow

Bede's world tells the remarkable story of the life and times of the Venerable Bede, 673–735 AD. Visitors can explore the origins of early medieval Northumbria and Bede's life and achievements through his own writings and the excavations of the monasteries at Jarrow and other sites.

Location – 10 miles from Newcastle upon Tyne, off the A19 near the southern entrance to the River Tyne tunnel. Bus services 526 & 527

Bede's World, Church Bank, Jarrow, Tyne and Wear, NE32 3DY
Tel. 0191 489 2106; Fax: 0191 428 2361; website: www.bedesworld.co.uk

Sutton Hoo near Woodbridge, Suffolk

Sutton Hoo is a group of low burial mounds overlooking the River Deben in south-east Suffolk. Excavations in 1939 brought to light the richest burial ever discovered in Britain – an Anglo-Saxon ship containing a magnificent treasure which has become one of the principal attractions of the British Museum. The mound from which the treasure was dug is thought to be the grave of Rædwald, an early English king who died in 624/5 AD.

This National Trust site has an excellent visitor centre, which includes a reconstruction of the burial chamber and its grave goods. Some original objects as well as replicas of the treasure are on display.

2 miles east of Woodbridge on B1083   Tel. 01394 389700

West Stow Anglo-Saxon Village

An early Anglo-Saxon Settlement reconstructed on the site where it was excavated consisting of timber and thatch hall, houses and workshop. There is also a museum containing objects found during the excavation of the site. Open all year 10am–4.15pm (except Yuletide). Special provision for school parties. A teachers' resource pack is available. Costumed events are held on some weekends, especially Easter Sunday and August Bank Holiday Monday. Craft courses are organised.

For further details see www.stedmunds.co.uk/west_stow.html or contact:
The Visitor Centre, West Stow Country Park, Icklingham Road, West Stow,
Bury St Edmunds, Suffolk IP28 6HG   Tel. 01284 728718